DINOSAUR ACTIVITY LAB

Senior editor Michelle Crane
Senior designer Stefan Podhorodecki
Illustrator Simon Tegg

Managing editor Francesca Baines
Managing art editor Phillip Letsu
Senior production editor Andy Hilliard
Senior production controller Jude Crozier
Jacket designer Stephanie Cheng Hui Tan
Design development manager Sophia MTT
Senior jackets coordinator Priyanka Sharma-Saddi
Jacket DTP designer Rakesh Kumar
Picture researcher Ahmad Bilal Khan

Publisher Andrew Macintyre
Art director Karen Self
Associate publishing director Liz Wheeler
Publishing director Jonathan Metcalf

Consultant Chris Barker
Photographer Nigel Wright

PRODUCED FOR DK BY:
XAB Design
Designers Nigel Wright, Jan Browne
Art direction Nigel Wright
Project creation Nigel Wright
Project editor Stephanie Farrow

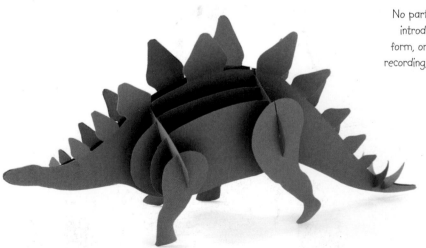

First published in Great Britain in 2022
by Dorling Kindersley Limited
DK, One Embassy Gardens,
8 Viaduct Gardens, London, SW11 7BW
The authorised representative in the EEA is Dorling Kindersley
Verlag GmbH. Arnulfstr. 124, 80636 Munich, Germany

Copyright © 2022 Dorling Kindersley Limited
A Penguin Random House Company
10 9 8 7 6 5 4 3 2 1
001–326773–October/2022

A CIP catalogue record for this book
is available from the British Library.
ISBN: 978-0-2415-3626-1

Printed and bound in China

For the curious
www.dk.com

This book was made with Forest Stewardship Council ™ certified paper
– one small step in DK's commitment to a sustainable future.
For more information go to
www.dk.com/our-green-pledge

DINOSAUR ACTIVITY
LAB

EXCITING PROJECTS FOR
BUDDING PALAEONTOLOGISTS

CONTENTS

STEM FACTS
This symbol highlights extra information that explains the learning behind a project.

PREHISTORIC FACTS
This symbol flags up extra information about life in the prehistoric world.

WARNING
This symbol identifies a task that might be dangerous. Be sure to get adult supervision.

A WORD ABOUT GLUES

Several of the projects in this book require the use of glue. We have suggested that you use ordinary PVA glue or glue sticks, but in some cases it will be easier to use a glue gun if you have one, as this glue dries much faster. A glue gun should only ever be used by an adult, and they must be sure to follow the manufacturer's guidelines.

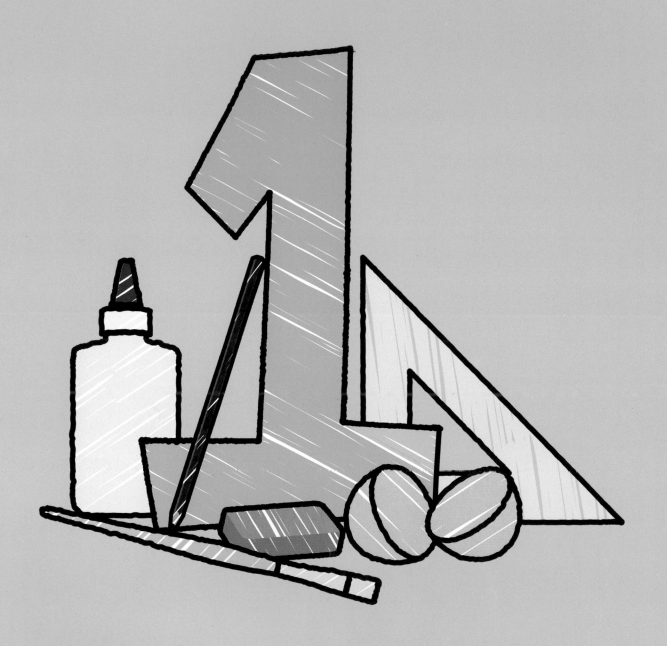

DINOSAUR FUN

In this chapter, you'll find fun projects to fill your world with prehistoric creatures, from flapping *Pteranodons* soaring overhead to dino-egg bath bombs that "hatch" tiny dinosaurs into the water. Build a *Triceratops* head that bursts through your wall, or make a mask and tail to become a *Tyrannosaurus*. Get measuring, cutting, folding, curling, gluing, slotting, taping, sewing, painting, squidging, stuffing, and building as you make these exciting dinosaur projects!

GLOWING WORLDS
PREHISTORIC LANTERN

Prehistoric creatures didn't all live at the same time, or in the same type of terrain. Which of your favourites lived alongside each other? Did they live in the forest, or ocean, or desert? You can make these glowing lanterns to recreate their worlds.

Think about scale (how big the shapes need to be in relation to each other).

Pliosaurs and other marine reptiles could "swim" around a deep blue ocean lantern.

Use a background colour to show water, forest, or desert, for example.

Make string handles for your lantern, or use it as a nightlight by your bed.

Cut out silhouettes of creatures, plants, and mountains.

MAKE YOUR OWN
PREHISTORIC LANTERN

This project shows you how to make a forest lantern, using a large jar and green tissue paper. To make a different one, just change the colour of the paper (blue for ocean, for example, or orange for a hot desert world) and research different template shapes.

Kentrosaurus

Time 90 minutes, plus drying time

Difficulty Easy

Tendaguripterus

Veterupristisaurus

WHAT YOU NEED

Green tissue paper

2 pieces of black paper (one big enough to go right round the jar)

Large glass jar approx. 18 cm (7 in) high and 9 cm (3½ in) across

PVA glue

Dicraeosaurus

Paintbrush

Pencil

String

Ruler

Scissors

Battery-powered tea light

Giraffatitan

TEMPLATES
For our lantern, we used the creatures above, which all shared the same habitat at the same time, but if you want, you can research your own favourites. Remember to keep the templates in proportion, so the silhouettes are the correct size compared to each other.

Rough, uneven squares will create interesting light effects.

1 Tear up a large sheet of tissue paper into small squares, about 2 cm x 2 cm (1 in x 1 in). Don't worry about making the squares neat.

2 Paint glue on a section of the inside of the jar and then use your brush to stick squares over the glue. Work on a small area at a time.

3 Smooth the paper down with more glue and overlap the edges so that there are no gaps between the squares.

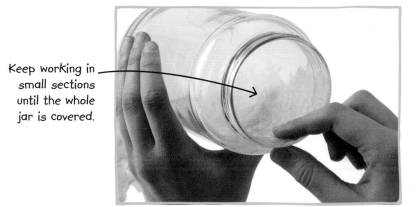

Keep working in small sections until the whole jar is covered.

4 When you get to the top of the jar, make sure you have a neat edge around the rim.

The overlapped squares of tissue paper create different strengths of colour.

5 Let the inside of the jar dry while you measure out your silhouettes.

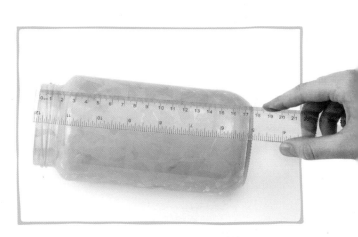

6 Measure the height of the jar and divide that measurement in half to determine how wide to make your strip of black paper.

7 Cut a strip of black paper as wide as the measurement in step 6, and long enough to fit round the jar with an overlap of about 1 cm (⅖ in).

Trim the strip of paper to length.

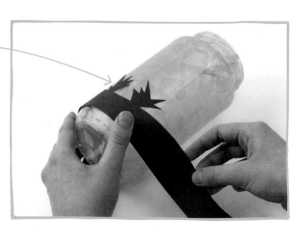

8 On the strip, sketch out the landscape you want for your prehistoric creatures. You could draw a few bushes, or even a hill.

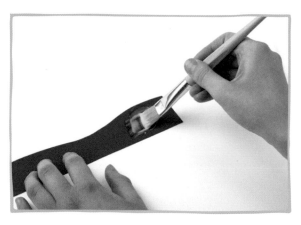

9 Cut out your strip of landscape and paint glue onto the back of it.

Some dinosaur plant foods, such as ferns, still grow on Earth today.

10 Stick the strip around the jar (near the base, but where the side is still flat).

If you find drawing difficult, trace the shapes instead, or use the grid method on page 17.

The huge neck of *Giraffatitan* accounted for half its total length.

12 Cut out the *Giraffatitan* silhouette. Paint glue onto the back of it and carefully add it to the scene.

11 Copy the template of the *Giraffatitan* onto black paper (remember to think about the scale of the dinosaur and the height of the jar).

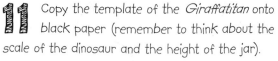

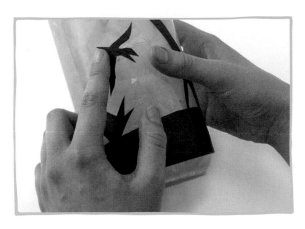

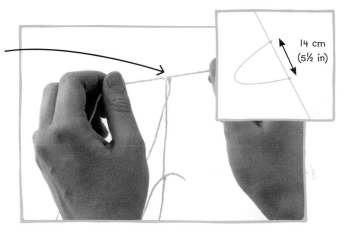

Tie each end of the handle loosely, so you can adjust later if necessary.

14 cm (5½ in)

13 Repeat steps 11–12 to copy the other silhouettes on page 10 and glue them around the side of the jar.

14 Cut a length of string 65 cm (24 in) long to go around the jar, and another 30 cm (12 in) long for the handle. Tie the ends of the handle to the long piece, about 14 cm (5½ in) apart.

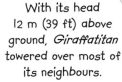

16 Hang the lantern up or put it by your bed for some dino-dreams.

15 Wrap the long piece of string twice around the neck of the jar and knot tightly. Adjust the handle knot positions if necessary, and then tighten. Switch on the tea light and place it inside.

With its head 12 m (39 ft) above ground, *Giraffatitan* towered over most of its neighbours.

PREHISTORIC WORLD
WHERE DID DINOSAURS LIVE?

Dinosaurs made their home in lots of different habitats across the planet, from arid desert plains and lush forests to even polar regions. Some lived along rivers or lakes, or roamed floodplains and swamps, while for others, coastal shores and lagoons provided the right kind of habitat.

JURASSIC GIANT
STEGOSAURUS WORLD

This armoured dinosaur lived 150–145 million years ago during the Jurassic Period. Using a clever grid technique to copy the shapes and make them bigger or smaller, you can build your own 3D *Stegosaurus* out of card, and create a mini Jurassic world too.

Many Jurassic trees were similar to the trees we have now.

Learn how to use scale to make your stegosaurs different sizes.

Cut out mountain shapes
in different colours to
make a backdrop.

Stegosaurus is famous
for the double row of
bony plates on its back.

Stegosaurus used
its spiked tail to
defend itself.

MAKE YOUR OWN
3D MODEL STEGOSAURUS

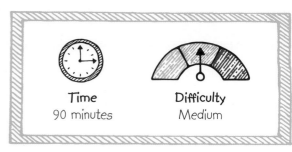

Time
90 minutes

Difficulty
Medium

The secret to scaling a shape is to draw a grid, so you can make something bigger or smaller while keeping everything in proportion. The scale factor is the amount you increase or decrease the size by. Here it is 1:4 – each 1 cm (²/₅ in) square on the template is equal to 4 cm (1½ in) on your grid. Afterwards, you can change the scale to create a herd of different-sized stegosaurs.

The squares on the template are 1 cm × 1 cm (²/₅ in × ²/₅ in).

WHAT YOU NEED

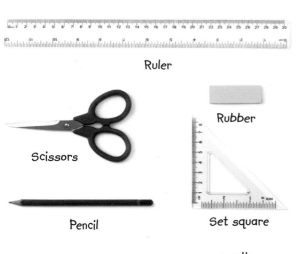

Ruler

Rubber

Scissors

Set square

Pencil

Marker pen

Double-sided adhesive tape

Coloured card

TEMPLATE 1

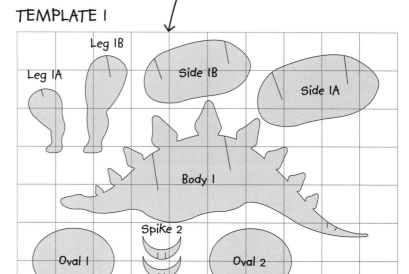

Leg 1B

Leg 1A

Side 1B

Side 1A

Body 1

Spike 2

Oval 1

Oval 2

Spike 1

TEMPLATE 2

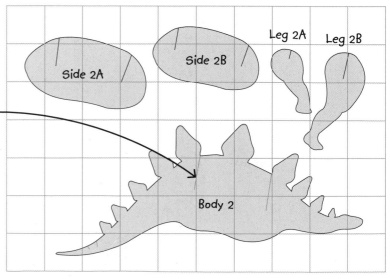

Side 2A

Side 2B

Leg 2A

Leg 2B

Body 2

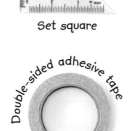

These straight lines show where you will need to cut slots into the shape.

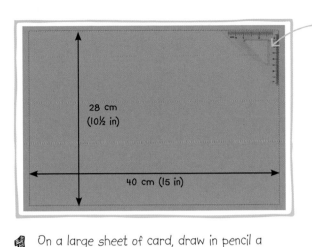

Using a set square will help you keep your corners at 90° right angles.

1 On a large sheet of card, draw in pencil a rectangle 40 cm (15 in) wide and 28 cm (10½ in) high.

2 Along the long and short edges of your rectangle, make marks every 4 cm (1½ in).

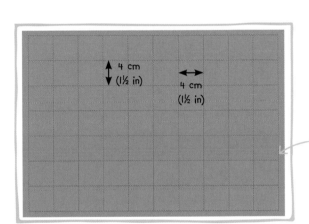

Working in small sections will help you copy each shape precisely.

The scale factor here is 1:4. Each square on the template is four times bigger on your grid.

3 Draw horizontal and vertical lines in pencil to join up the marks and create a grid of 10 squares across and 7 down. Use the set square to check the lines are all at right angles.

4 With a pen (or pencil if you prefer), copy the shapes on Template 1 accurately onto the card. Working one square at a time, use the gridlines to help you copy the shapes and slots of the template.

5 When you have copied all the shapes on Template 1, lightly label them in pencil so you know what they are once they're cut out. Then, on a second piece of card, repeat steps 1-5 to draw the shapes and slots on Template 2.

The gridlines will help you copy the shape accurately.

Remember to include the slot lines, and position them carefully.

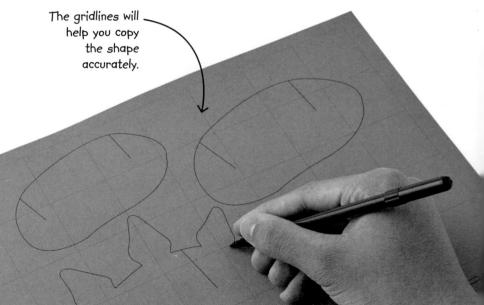

To find the middle, draw a line across the widest part and then the longest; where they cross is your centre point.

6 Rub out the pencil gridlines. Carefully cut out each shape along the pen lines., then cut the slots where marked. You could cut each piece out roughly first, so it is easier to work with.

7 Draw a line lengthways down the middle of Oval 1. Make a first mark 6 mm (¼ in) from one end of the line, then mark every 10 mm (²/₅ in). You should have 6 mm (¼ in) left.

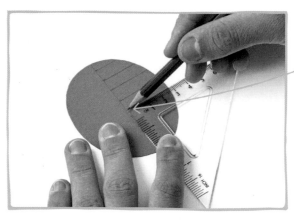

Use a set square to keep all eight lines parallel with each other.

8 Position a set square on the line and, at each mark, draw a line at right angles across to the edge. You should have eight lines in total.

9 Cut along each of those lines to the centre line, making sure you don't cut too far. Then repeat steps 7–9 for Oval 2.

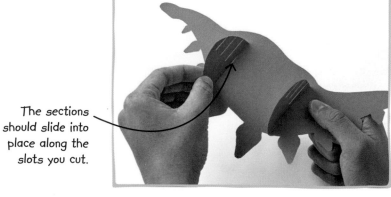

The sections should slide into place along the slots you cut.

10 Slide Oval 1 into the "slot" of Body 1 nearest the tail, using the fourth slot of the oval.

11 Ease the fourth slot of Oval 2 into the slot of Body 1 nearest the head. Push gently to make sure they are both firmly in place.

The bony plates on *Stegosaurus* may have helped it look bigger than it was, to deter predators.

12 Position Side 1A so that the two slots in it line up with the third slots in the ovals. Ease Side 1A into both ovals at the same time.

13 Repeat step 12, but this time with Side 1B, sliding it carefully into the second slots of the two ovals.

Hold the model carefully as you build the second side.

14 Slide Leg 1A into the final slot of Oval 2 and Leg 1B into the final slot of Oval 1. That's the first half of your dinosaur done!

15 Turn the model over and slide Body 2 into the fifth slot of the two ovals, making sure the head faces the same way as it does on Body 1.

Your 2D pieces of card are locking together to make a 3D dinosaur.

16 Repeat steps 12–13 with the other two side pieces, building up the body of your *Stegosaurus*.

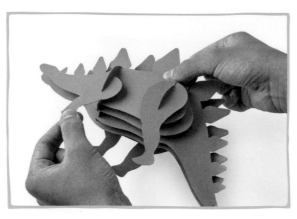

Stegosaurus had a very flexible tail that could swing in large arcs.

17 As for step 14, slide Leg 2B into Oval 1 and Leg 2A into Oval 2.

18 Ease the legs up or down slightly within the slots to balance your *Stegosaurus* so it can stand upright.

Stick the head ends of the two body pieces together.

19 Join the two head ends of Body 1 and Body 2 with a small piece of double-sided adhesive tape or a dab of glue.

20 Slide the Spike 1 piece into the two slots nearest the tail end of the main body pieces. Slide Spike 2 into the two remaining slots.

21 Finally, gently bend the "plates" slightly away from the centre on both sides.

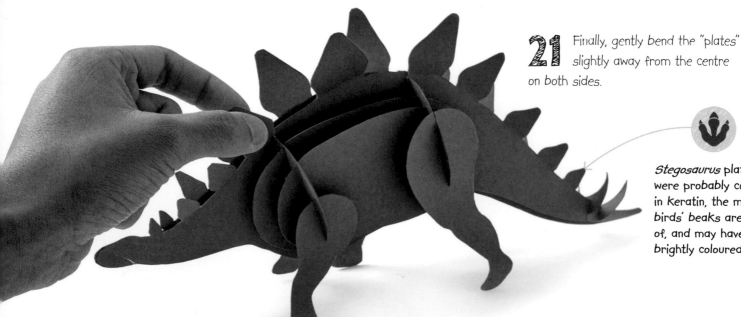

Stegosaurus plates were probably covered in keratin, the material birds' beaks are made of, and may have been brightly coloured.

FEED YOUR HERD

Stegosaurs were herbivores (plant-eaters), so you could make a whole forest of Jurassic trees for your herd to eat. Start with a grid of 5 cm (2 in) squares, then change the scale to make trees of different sizes.

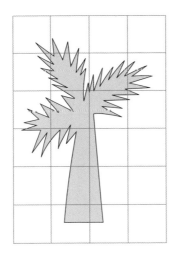
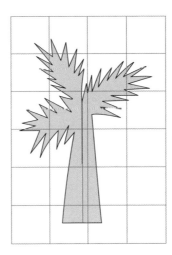

1 Draw a grid of 5 cm (2 in) squares and copy the template above onto your grid twice.

2 Mark the red and black slots as shown, then cut out both pieces. Rub out the grid marks.

3 Cut the red slot on one piece and the black slot on the other, then slide them together.

PREHISTORIC WORLD
DINOSAUR DEFENCES

Just like animals today, dinosaurs needed defence strategies. For a few, size alone was enough to put off predators; others were small enough to hide, or lived in groups for protection. Some relied on speed; others on inbuilt weaponry such as horns, claws, and clubbed or spiked tails. These weapons weren't just for fighting off meat-eaters, though, they were often adaptations to secure mates and resources too.

A blow from the club on the tail of an *Ankylosaurus* could shatter an attacker's bones.

Struthiomimus relied not on armour but on speed to outrun many of its predators.

Kentrosaurus was heavily armoured and could use its spiked tail as a weapon.

Styracosaurus had an impressive set of horns and a defensive neck frill.

DINOSAUR HAND PUPPETS

Dinosaurs' teeth evolved to suit their diet. Those of a herbivore such as *Psittacosaurus* could cut up vegetation, while those of a carnivore such as a *Velociraptor* were more like blades for slicing meat. Why not make one of each?

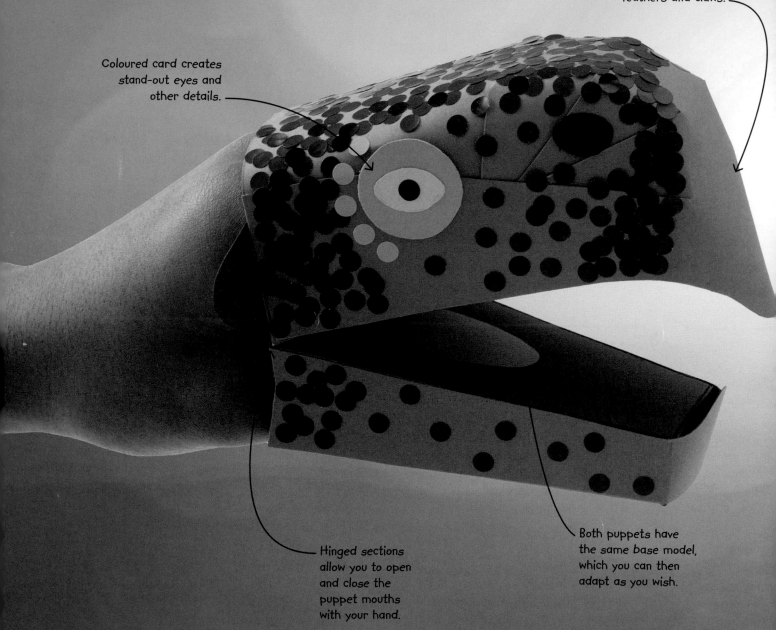

The *Psittacosaurus* beak was covered in keratin, the same material that makes up feathers and claws.

Coloured card creates stand-out eyes and other details.

Hinged sections allow you to open and close the puppet mouths with your hand.

Both puppets have the same base model, which you can then adapt as you wish.

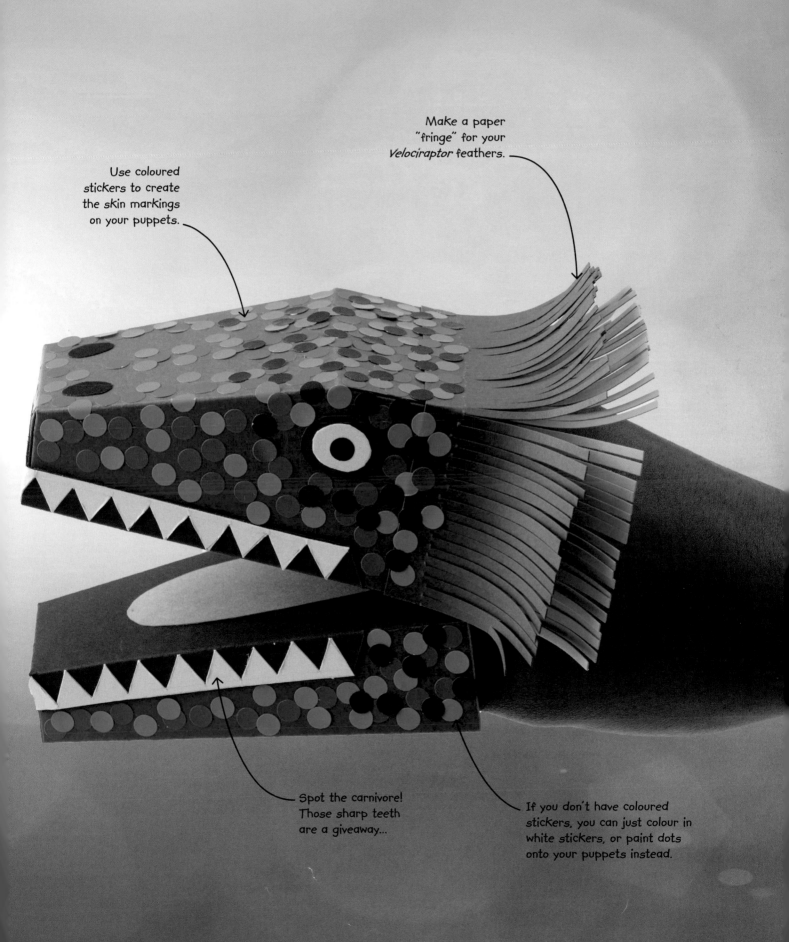

Make a paper "fringe" for your *Velociraptor* feathers.

Use coloured stickers to create the skin markings on your puppets.

Spot the carnivore! Those sharp teeth are a giveaway...

If you don't have coloured stickers, you can just colour in white stickers, or paint dots onto your puppets instead.

MAKE YOUR OWN
HAND PUPPETS

Both puppets are made with the same basic template pieces below, but are then adapted in different ways to make the two dinosaurs. Use the grid method on page 17 to copy the template shapes, with a scale of 1:2.

WHAT YOU NEED

Pencil

Scissors

Paintbrush

Coloured card

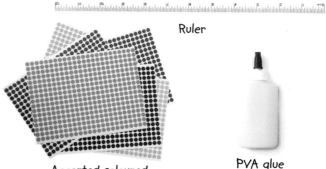

Ruler

PVA glue

Assorted coloured circle-shaped stickers

BASIC TEMPLATES

Each 2 cm (¾ in) square on this template is equal to 4 cm (1½ in) on your grid.

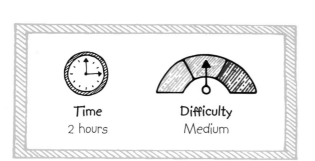

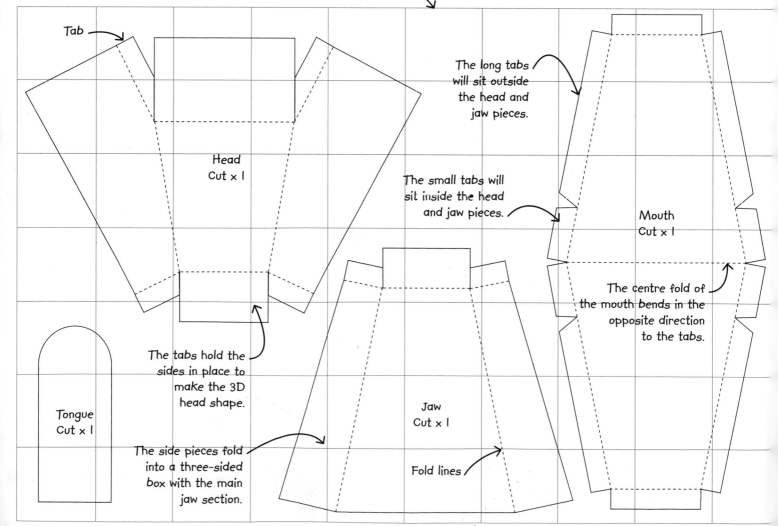

Tab

Head
Cut x 1

The long tabs will sit outside the head and jaw pieces.

The small tabs will sit inside the head and jaw pieces.

Mouth
Cut x 1

The centre fold of the mouth bends in the opposite direction to the tabs.

The tabs hold the sides in place to make the 3D head shape.

Tongue
Cut x 1

Jaw
Cut x 1

Fold lines

The side pieces fold into a three-sided box with the main jaw section.

Time
2 hours

Difficulty
Medium

MAKE A VELOCIRAPTOR

1 Copy the head and jaw template shapes onto the card you've chosen, scaling them up to double their size. Then cut them out.

We used green card for the head and jaw.

2 Carefully crease along each of the fold lines on the head piece, bending all the tabs and sides in the same direction.

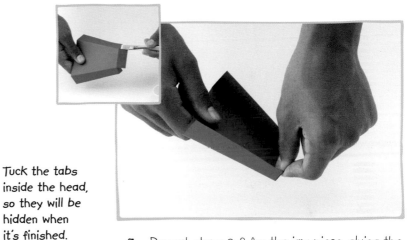

3 Apply glue to the tabs on the head piece, then stick them to the inside of the two rectangular sections at either end of the head piece.

Tuck the tabs inside the head, so they will be hidden when it's finished.

4 Repeat steps 2–3 for the jaw piece, gluing the tabs to the rectangular section at one end of it to make a three-sided box shape.

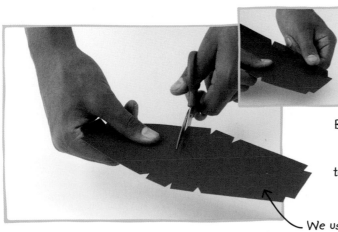

Brush glue on the outside of the two tabs near the centre fold.

We used dark red card for the mouth.

5 Copy the mouth template onto your card and cut it out. Bend it along the centre fold in one direction, then fold all the tabs the opposite way.

6 Working on one half of the mouth piece, apply glue to the inside of the three larger tabs, and to the outside of the two smaller tabs.

The centre fold in the mouth piece becomes a hinge.

Hold the pieces together until the glue has set firmly.

7 Position the glued tabs over the jaw piece, with the three larger tabs on the outside and the two smaller tabs tucked inside. Stick them together.

8 Repeat steps 6–7 to attach the other half of the mouth piece to the head piece, following the same positioning for the tabs.

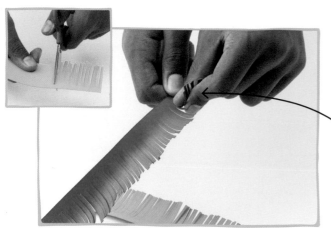

Curl the fringes gently with your fingers to "feather" them.

9 For the fringe, cut two strips of paper 5 cm x 17 cm (2 in x 6¾ in); we made one dark green and one light green. Snip parallel cuts along each strip, about three-quarters of the way across them.

10 Glue the non-fringed edges of each strip around the head piece. Overlap them but stick the upper strip about 1 cm (²/₅ in) further away from the edge than the lower strip.

Velociraptor teeth were serrated to tear flesh.

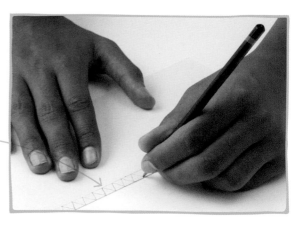

11 To make the tongue, copy the template shape onto pink card. Cut it out, and then glue it to the lower side of the mouth piece.

12 Draw a line 23 cm (9 in) long, 1 cm (²/₅ in) from the edge of a piece of cream card. Between the edge and the line, draw a row of zig-zag teeth.

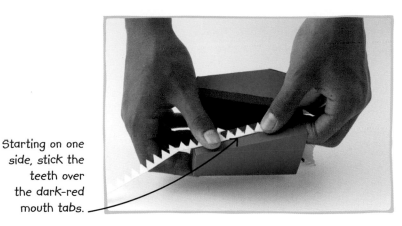

Starting on one side, stick the teeth over the dark-red mouth tabs.

13 Carefully cut out the row of teeth, then repeat steps 12–13 to make a second row of teeth for the upper side of the mouth.

14 Glue one row of teeth carefully over the mouth tabs around the jaw piece. Then stick the other row of teeth around the upper jaw.

Make "pupils" by sticking black dots on the cream ovals.

15 For the eyes, stick two black dots on some cream card. Draw an oval around each one and cut them out.

16 Draw and cut out two slightly larger ovals on dark-red card. Stick the cream ovals onto the red ones, and glue them onto the head.

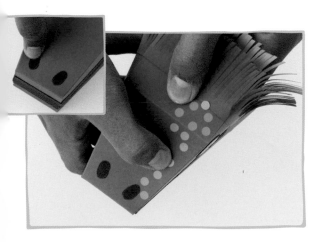

Add darker-coloured dots towards the back of the head.

Keep the pattern random and overlap the dots sometimes.

17 For the nostrils, cut two small ovals from black card and glue them to the top of the head. Then begin dotting on green stickers.

18 Build up layers of dots to create the skin pattern. Then slide your hand inside the puppet to let your *Velociraptor* go and hunt for prey...

ADDITIONAL TEMPLATES

These extra shapes are needed for the *Psittacosaurus.*

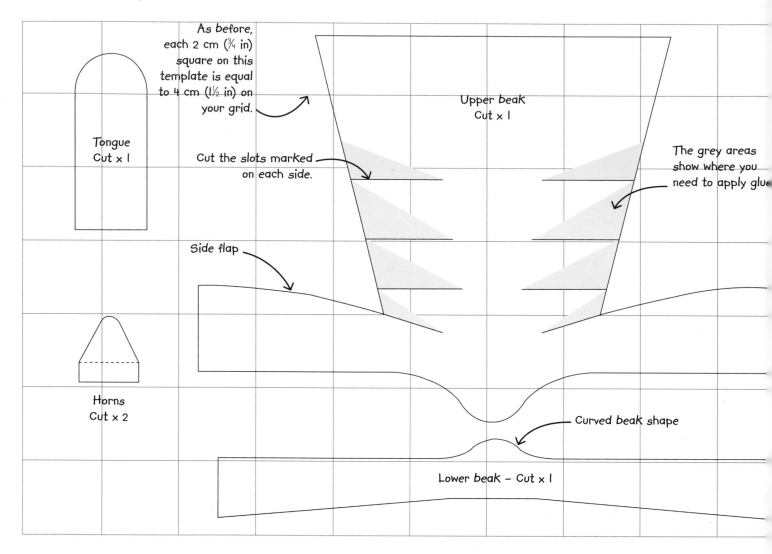

As before, each 2 cm (¾ in) square on this template is equal to 4 cm (1½ in) on your grid.

Tongue
Cut x 1

Cut the slots marked on each side.

Upper beak
Cut x 1

The grey areas show where you need to apply glue

Side flap

Horns
Cut x 2

Curved beak shape

Lower beak – Cut x 1

MAKE A PSITTACOSAURUS

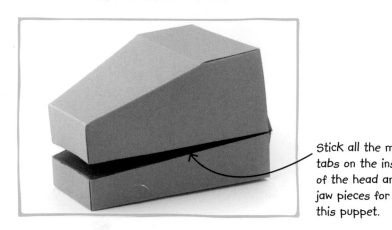

Stick all the mouth tabs on the inside of the head and jaw pieces for this puppet.

1 Follow steps 1–8 on pages 25–26 to make the base head, but only use brown card instead of green and red, and glue all the tabs inside the head.

2 Copy the upper and lower beak templates onto brown card. Cut them out, including the straight slots marked on the upper beak piece.

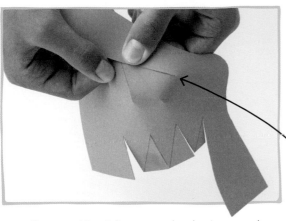

Stick the side flap over the top, to hide all the triangles.

Start with the slot nearest the side flap.

3 On one side of the upper *beak* piece, apply glue to the areas marked on the template. Tuck the glued triangles behind the straight cuts, one at a time, and hold in place.

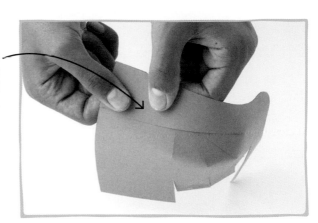

4 Once all the triangles are secure, line up the side flap with the *back edge* of the upper *beak* piece and glue it in place. Hold until the glue has set.

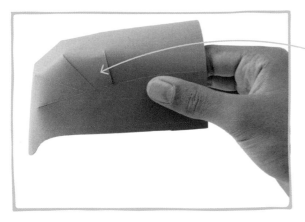

The name *Psittacosaurus* means "parrot lizard", after its pointy beak.

5 Next, repeat steps 3–4 on the other side of the upper *beak* piece, to give you a domed beak shape with *both side flaps* on the outside.

6 Apply glue to both sides of the upper section of the base head you made in step 1.

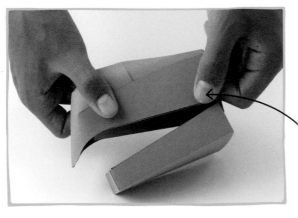

Press the side flaps to glue them to the sides of the base head.

7 Stick the upper *beak* piece to the glued sides of the upper section, pressing gently until the glue has set.

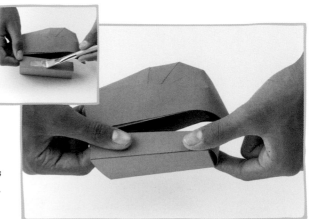

8 Apply glue to the jaw section of the *base head*. Stick the lower *beak* piece to it, with the curved *beak* shape facing upwards. Hold until set.

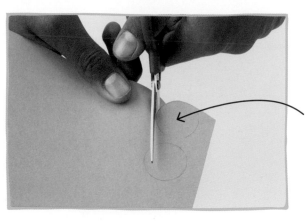

You could draw round a coin to make your circles.

9 For the eyes, draw two circles about 2.5 cm (1 in) in diameter on pink card. Then cut out the two circles.

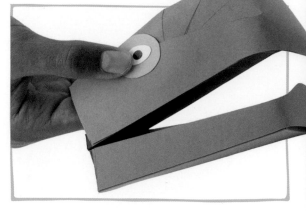

10 Next, cut out two smaller ovals of yellow card. Glue the ovals onto the pink circles, add two black dots for "pupils", and glue onto either side of the head.

11 For the nostrils, cut two small oval shapes out of black card and glue them on either side of the beak, as shown.

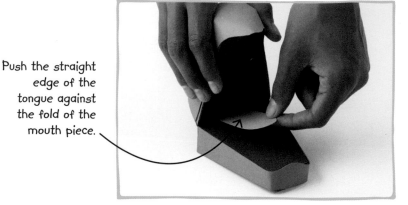

Push the straight edge of the tongue against the fold of the mouth piece.

12 Draw and cut out a tongue from pink card, using the template on page 28. Glue it in position on the lower mouth piece.

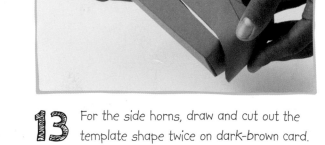

Glue the tabs inside the head piece, just above the mouth hinge, one on either side.

13 For the side horns, draw and cut out the template shape twice on dark-brown card. Fold along the tab lines, and glue the tabs in place.

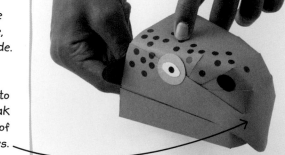

Remember to keep the beak area free of stickers.

14 Start creating your *Psittacosaurus* skin pattern by first dotting brown stickers randomly over the head.

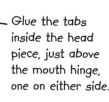

Too small to be used for defence, the side horns were probably for attracting a mate.

16 Add deeper-coloured stickers to create darker areas around the beak and side horns. Then put your hand inside and find some leaves for your *Psittacosaurus* to chomp.

15 Add some pink stickers around the back of the eyes, as shown, to echo the card colour you used in step 9.

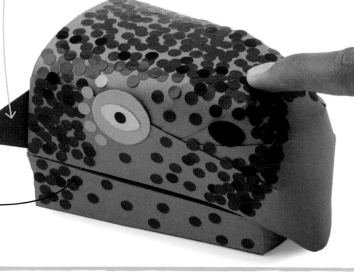

Don't forget to put stickers on the lower jaw as well as the top of the head.

PREHISTORIC WORLD
EAT LIKE A HERBIVORE

The narrow, parrot-like beak that gave *Psittacosaurus* its name would have been used to slice off vegetation, which it would then have shredded with its small, sharp teeth. The beak may also have been used to gather seeds, and was tough enough to be put to use as a nutcracker. It might even have been used to give enemies a nasty bite!

EAT LIKE A CARNIVORE

In its long, narrow snout, *Velociraptor* had jaws filled with teeth that were perfectly evolved for ripping meat off bones and carving through flesh. It had up to 56 extremely sharp teeth, each of which was a back-curved blade with serrated edges. Like most dinosaurs, the teeth were constantly replaced, so they never got blunt.

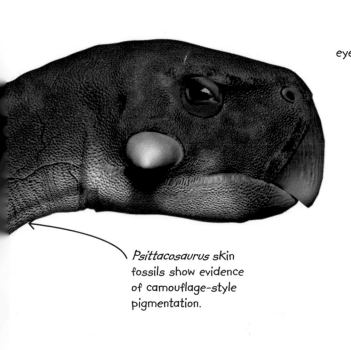

Psittacosaurus skin fossils show evidence of camouflage-style pigmentation.

Velociraptor's large eyes may have helped it spot small prey.

Its thought *Velociraptor* probably had extensive plumage.

TRICERATOPS WALL ART

Could a *Triceratops* stick its head through your bedroom wall? Very possibly! The skull of a *Triceratops* was one of the biggest and strongest of all dinosaur skulls. Its distinctive head frill and horns were all made of solid bone, but you can make this cardboard version to hang on your wall.

With careful measuring and cutting out, you can turn 2D card into a fearsome 3D head covered in horns and spikes.

A fringe of spikes along its frill made this young *Triceratops* look even more impressive.

Paint scaly
skin on your
Triceratops frill.

Triceratops had
a parrot-like beak and
lots of teeth for snipping
off and grinding low-
growing vegetation.

MAKE YOUR OWN
WALL-MOUNTED TRICERATOPS HEAD

This head is made from four pieces of stiff card, cut to form the jaw, beak, frill, and face. The three horns are made with thinner card. Carefully measure out the lines and angles to draw 2D shapes that slot together to make a 3D head.

Time 2 hours, plus painting time

Difficulty Hard

WHAT YOU NEED

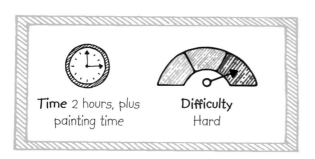

White thin card

Protractor

Pencil

Scissors

Stiff card

Ruler

String

Set square

Paintbrushes

Acrylic paints in a selection of colours

Plasticine

Masking tape

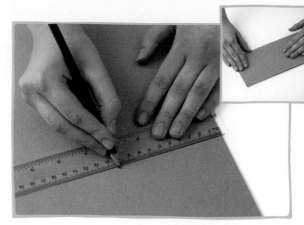

1 First, make the jaw. Measure and cut a strip of stiff card 10 cm x 42 cm (4 in x 16½ in), then fold it in half so it's 21 cm (8¼ in) long.

25°

2 At the non-folded end, mark a 25°-angle and draw a line through it from the corner to the opposite edge. Cut both layers of card on that line.

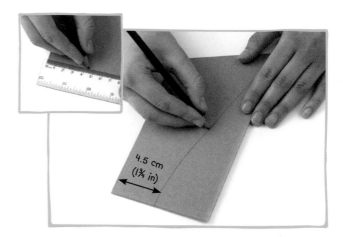

4.5 cm (1¾ in)

3 At the folded end, mark 4.5 cm (1¾ in) from the shortest side. Draw a curved line from the mark to the far corner of the non-folded end.

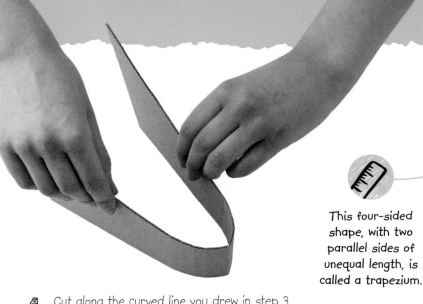

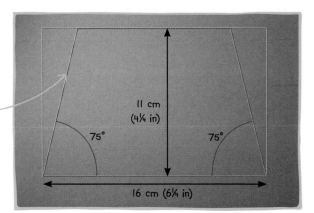

This four-sided shape, with two parallel sides of unequal length, is called a trapezium.

4 Cut along the curved line you drew in step 3, and then unfold the card. Bend it into a soft, rounded curve to form the shape of the jaw.

5 Draw a rectangle 16 cm x 11 cm (6¼ in x 4¼ in) onto stiff card. At each corner of one of the long edges, draw a line up at an angle of 75° to make a trapezium. Cut out the trapezium.

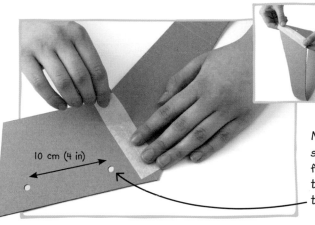

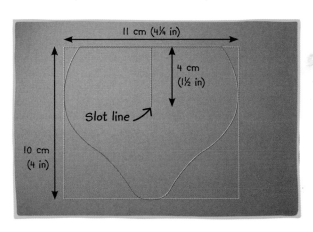

Make two holes as shown, 3 cm (1¼ in) from the edges, to thread string through in step 35.

6 Make two holes in the card with a pencil. Line up the trapezium's short side with the jaw's straight side. Tape the angled sides of both pieces together.

7 To make the beak, measure a rectangle 11 cm x 10 cm (4¼ in x 4 in). Inside it, sketch the shape shown above. At the mid-point on the flat edge, mark a slot 4 cm (1½ in) long.

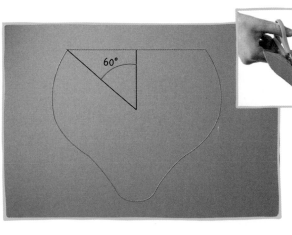

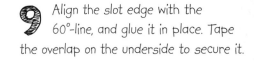

Overlapping the 2D shape along the 60°-line turns it into a 3D cone.

8 Draw a diagonal line at an angle of 60° from the central end of the slot line. Cut out the full shape, then cut along the vertical slot line.

9 Align the slot edge with the 60°-line, and glue it in place. Tape the overlap on the underside to secure it.

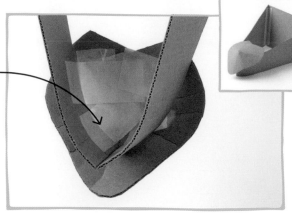

Make sure the beak is attached securely.

10 On the top edge of the jaw (the curved edge), fix some over-length pieces of tape, ready to attach the beak.

11 Stick the beak cone to the tape on the jaw, with the overlapping section of beak towards the back. Add more tape if necessary.

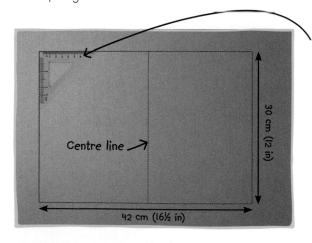

3.5 cm (1⅓ in)

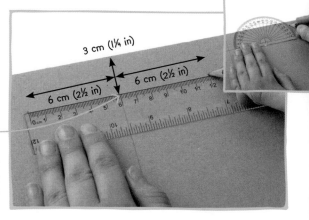

These slots will support the frill of your *Triceratops.*

12 Measure 3.5 cm (1⅓ in) from the back join of the jaw and cut a 2 cm (¾ in) slot from the top edge.

13 Repeat step 12 on the opposite side, so you have two 2 cm- (¾ in-) long slots, one on either side of the top of the jaw.

Use a set square to make sure your corners are at right angles.

Centre line →

30 cm (12 in)

42 cm (16½ in)

The centre line is at right angles to your baseline and bisects it.

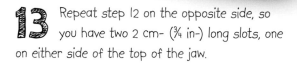

3 cm (1¼ in)

6 cm (2½ in)

6 cm (2½ in)

14 To make the frill, draw a rectangle 30 cm × 42 cm (12 in x 16½ in) on stiff card. Draw a vertical centre line down the middle, as shown. Cut out the rectangle.

15 Draw a baseline 6 cm (2½ in) either side of the centre line, 3 cm (1¼ in) down from the top edge. From either end of that baseline, draw a line at 25° across to the top edge.

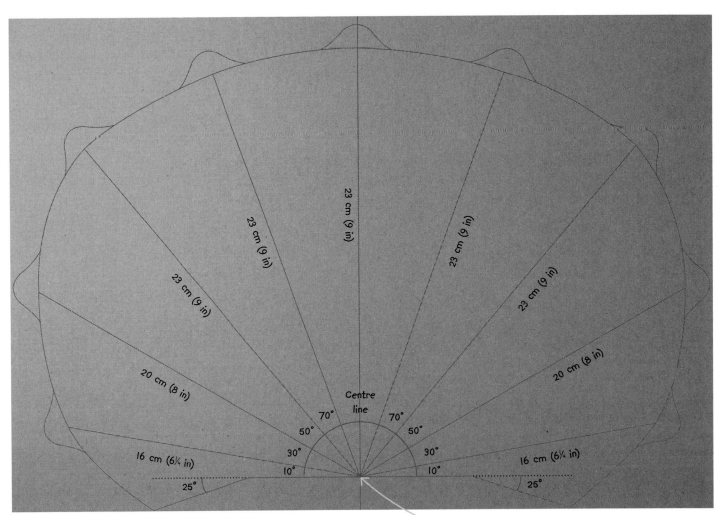

23 cm (9 in)

23 cm (9 in)

23 cm (9 in)

23 cm (9 in)

23 cm (9 in)

20 cm (8 in)

20 cm (8 in)

16 cm (6¼ in)

16 cm (6¼ in)

Centre line

70° 70°

50° 50°

30° 30°

10° 10°

25° 25°

16 Turn the card around so the baseline is at the bottom. Then copy the shape above, drawing radial lines at the angles and lengths shown. Draw a spike at the end of each line. Cut around the outline of the whole shape.

Lines that all start from a central point are called radial lines.

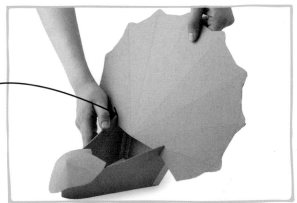

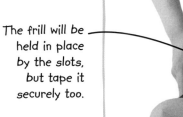

The frill will be held in place by the slots, but tape it securely too.

17 Hold a ruler against each radial line in turn and lift the card up gently to neatly crease the card. Bend the whole frill slightly to give it a backwards curve.

18 Push the frill into the slots you cut on the top of the jaw in steps 12–13, and use tape to secure it to the jaw strip from behind.

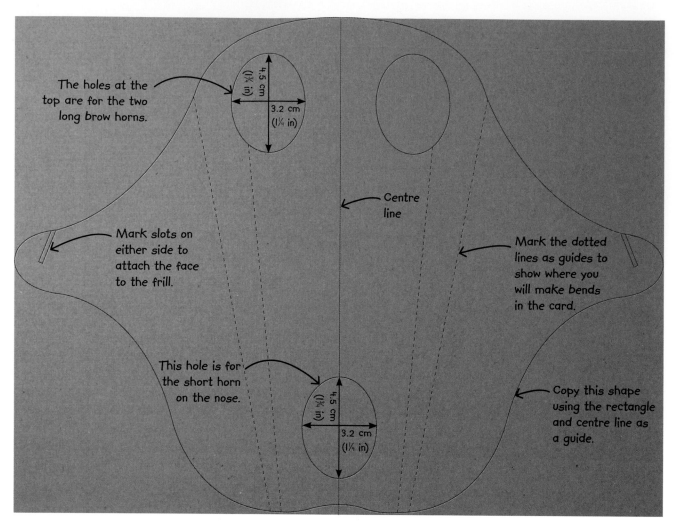

The holes at the top are for the two long brow horns.

4.5 cm (1¾ in)

3.2 cm (1¼ in)

Centre line

Mark slots on either side to attach the face to the frill.

Mark the dotted lines as guides to show where you will make bends in the card.

This hole is for the short horn on the nose.

4.5 cm (1¾ in)

3.2 cm (1¼ in)

Copy this shape using the rectangle and centre line as a guide.

19 To make the face, cut a rectangle 22 cm x 28 cm (8¾ in x 11 in). Draw a centre line vertically down it at 14 cm (5½ in), then sketch the shapes shown above in it. (Use the grid method on page 17 if you want help with this.)

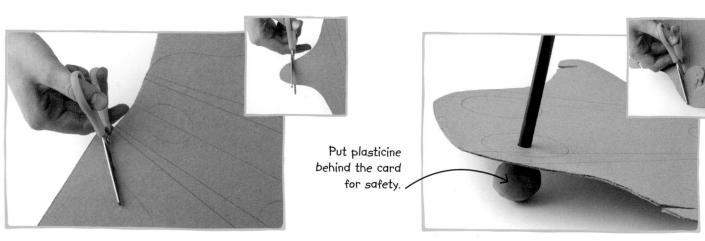

Put plasticine behind the card for safety.

20 Carefully cut out the face shape, including the slots on either side.

21 Cut the ovals for the horns. Push a pencil through the card first to make a hole through the centre of the ovals, and then cut carefully around the lines.

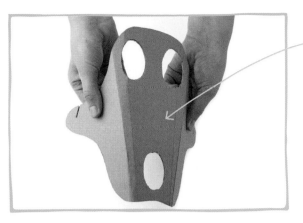

22 Hold a ruler against one of the dotted fold lines and lift the card up gently to make a crease. Repeat for the other three fold lines.

Injuries on *Triceratops* skull fossils suggest they may have locked horns and gouged each others' faces.

23 To make the small front horn, draw a baseline 8 cm (3 in) long on a piece of thin white card.

These are the measurements for the small horn.

8 cm (3 in)

Line up your protractor with the left end of the baseline.

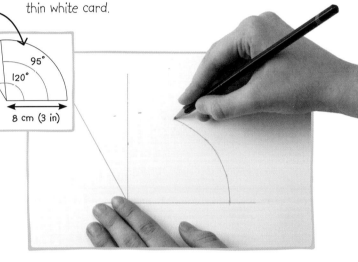

24 Mark off angles of 120° and 95° from the left end of the baseline. Draw two lines up from the left end – one line through each mark.

25 Mark a series of points 8 cm (3 in) from the left end and join them up into a curve. Cut along the baseline, curve, and 120°-line.

Triceratops' horns had a solid bone core with a tough outer casing.

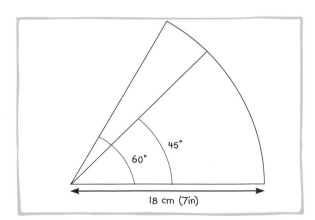

26 Roll the card into a cone, overlapping the baseline edge to meet the 95°-line you drew. Secure it with masking tape.

27 To make the two larger horns, follow steps 23–26, but this time using a baseline of 18 cm (7 in) and angles of 60° and 45°. Draw two.

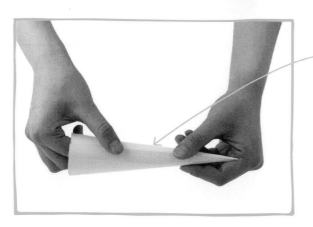

The two sharp-tipped brow horns were up to 1.3 m (4 ft) long.

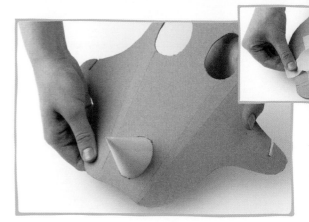

28 Cut both horns out, and curve them into cones so that the *baseline* edges overlap with the 45°-lines. Secure them with masking tape.

29 Push the small horn through the lower hole on the face and *secure* with masking tape on the *back*.

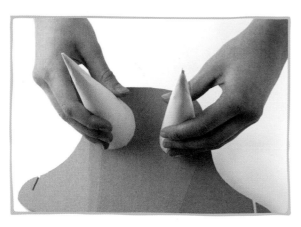

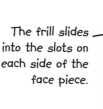

The frill slides into the slots on each side of the face piece.

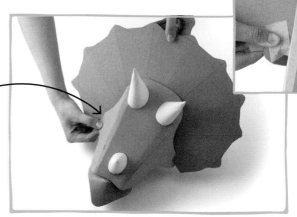

30 Position the two brow horns so that they point slightly outwards. Secure in place as for step 29.

31 Position the face piece over the jaw and *beak*. Slide the slots on either side of the face up into the frill, and tape it in place on the *back*.

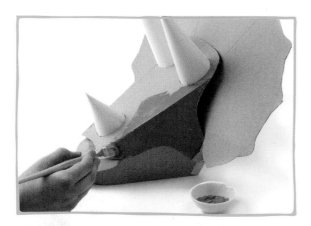

Triceratops' neck frill was made of solid bone covered in scaly skin.

32 Paint the head with a green *base* coat and the horns, spikes, and beak with a cream one. Once dry, paint a pinky edge around the frill, face, and *base* of the horns.

33 Dapple dark-green scaly skin markings along the radial lines, with pale brown strokes in between. Paint brown strokes halfway up the spikes, too, as shown.

Paint the horns the same colour as the frill spikes.

Only young *Triceratops* had bony spikes on their frill; as they grew older, the spikes smoothed over.

34 Paint dark- and mid-brown strokes onto the upper beak cone, as shown, and paint a matching semicircular lower beak directly onto the jaw strip.

35 Paint the horns, eyes, and nostrils, and brush pale brown strokes around the face. Once dry, thread a loop of string through the two holes you made in step 6, and hang the head up on your bedroom wall.

PREHISTORIC WORLD HIDDEN CLUES

How do we know that *Triceratops* had scaly skin, horns, and a frill? Fossils can't tell us what a dinosaur's skin, colouring, or feathers were like, can it? Well, actually, yes – to some degree. Fossils of *Triceratops* skin prints show that it had scales, some of which were large and pointed. Because the horns and frill were made of very strong solid bone, they have often survived when other parts of the dead animal simply rotted away.

Fossils of skin prints show that *Triceratops* had scaly skin.

SEW CLEVER
PLESIOSAUR KEYRING

Dinosaurs may have ruled the land on prehistoric Earth, but marine reptiles ruled the seas. Plesiosaurs were the marine giants of the waters, but this plesiosaur toy keyring is small enough to hang from a pocket or bag.

Choose a contrasting thread for the blanket stitch along the back.

Some plesiosaurs had more than 70 bones making up their long, snake-like necks.

A plesiosaur's long flippers could probably generate high speeds in short bursts.

MAKE YOUR OWN
FELT KEYRING

Felt is perfect for this project, because the fibres don't fray, so your plesiosaur won't come upurl. Don't worry if you're new to sewing; you'll find a guide to the stitches used on page 47.

Time 60 minutes, plus drying time

Difficulty Medium

WHAT YOU NEED

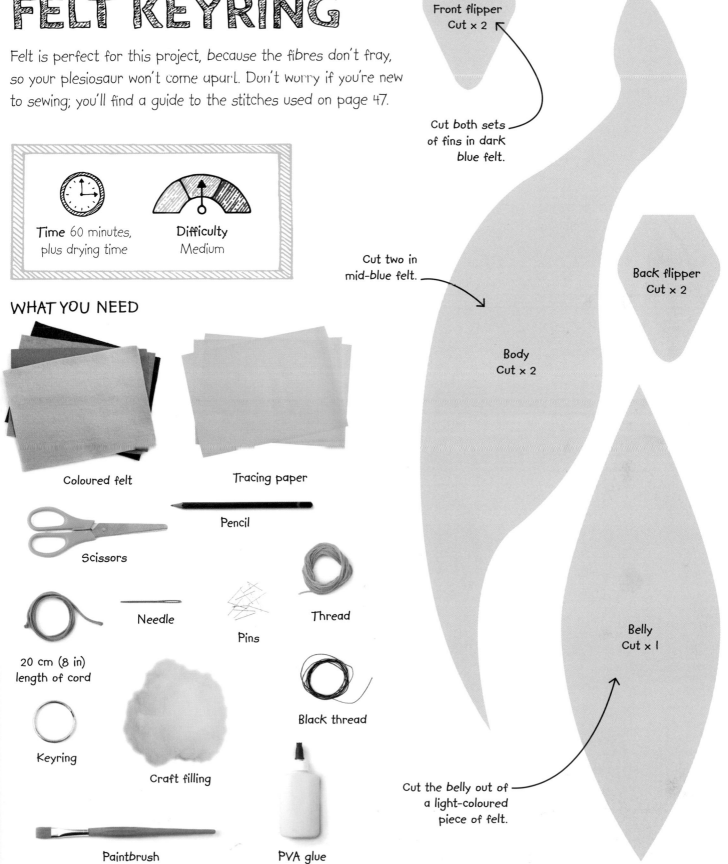

Coloured felt

Tracing paper

Pencil

Scissors

Needle

Thread

Pins

20 cm (8 in) length of cord

Keyring

Craft filling

Black thread

Paintbrush

PVA glue

TEMPLATES

Front flipper
Cut x 2

Cut both sets of fins in dark blue felt.

Back flipper
Cut x 2

Cut two in mid-blue felt.

Body
Cut x 2

Belly
Cut x 1

Cut the belly out of a light-coloured piece of felt.

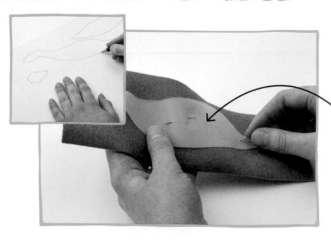

1 Trace the templates onto tracing paper and cut them out. Pin the body shape onto *blue felt*, and cut around it. Repeat to make a second body piece.

Pin the tracing paper in position to help you cut accurately.

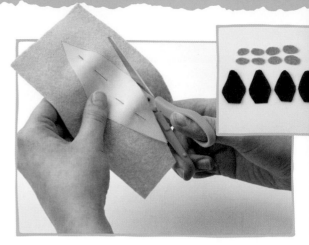

2 Pin the belly shape onto *grey felt* and the flippers onto *dark-blue felt*. Cut around them, then cut out eight orange ovals for body markings.

3 Line up the flat edge of a front flipper along the belly edge of a body piece, towards the head end, and a back flipper nearer the tail end.

Pale bellies may have camouflaged plesiosaurs in the water.

4 Position the belly piece over the top of the flippers. Pin through the *belly*, *flippers*, and *body* piece to hold them all in place.

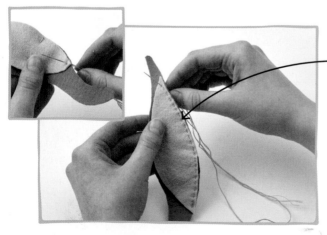

This stitching will be on the inside when the keyring is finished.

This side will be on the outside when the keyring is finished.

5 Use running stitch to sew the belly to the body piece, including the flippers, as the seam will fix the pieces together. Make a finishing knot.

6 Turn the felt round the right way so you can see the outside. Check the flippers are firmly secured; add a few more stitches on the inside if not.

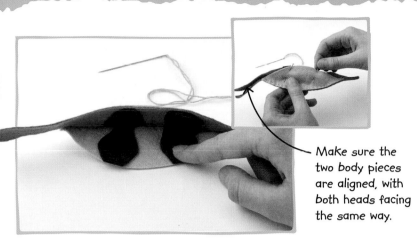

Make sure the two body pieces are aligned, with both heads facing the same way.

7 Turn the felt inside out. Position the two other flippers on the inside unsewn belly edge, and line up the second body piece along it, on top of them.

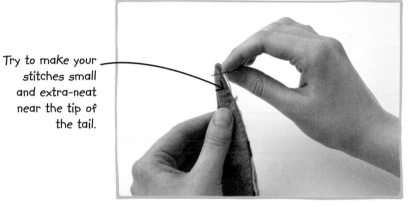

8 Starting at the tail end, use running stitch to sew along the belly, attaching both it and the two flippers to the second body piece.

Try to make your stitches small and extra-neat near the tip of the tail.

9 Continue stitching to join the two body pieces along the neck. Make a finishing knot once you reach the end of the neck, before the head.

10 Using running stitch again, sew the other end of the two body pieces together, from the belly piece to the tip of the tail.

11 Once more, open out your plesiosaur to make sure the flippers are securely in place.

Plesiosaurs probably flapped their flippers up and down to "fly" through the water.

If a flipper doesn't feel secure, sew a few extra stitches along its seam.

This seam is on the outside of the felt, while the belly seams are hidden inside.

12 Blanket-stitch the two body pieces together along the plesiosaur's back, beginning at the tip of the tail.

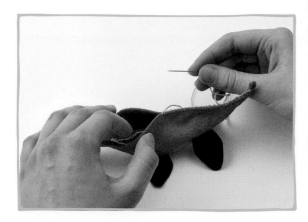

13 Continue sewing until you reach a point about midway along the back, then pause – this is where you are going to insert the keyring.

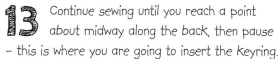

Pull the ends through the loop to attach the cord.

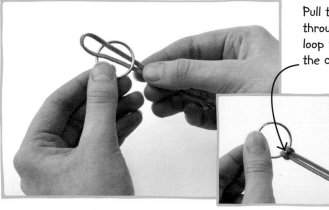

14 Fold your cord in half. Push the looped end through the keyring, thread the ends back through the loop and pull them to secure the keyring on the cord.

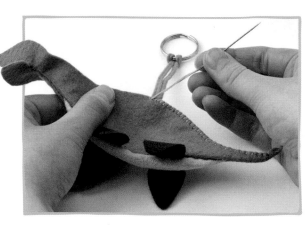

15 Tuck both ends of the cord between the two body pieces, leaving the keyring about 5 cm (2 in) above the back seam. Blanket-stitch it in place and make a finishing knot.

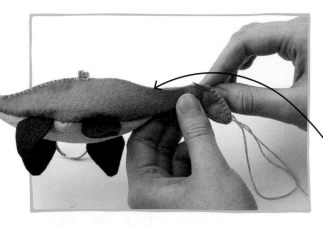

Sew only part-way along the spine, to leave an opening for stuffing.

16 Blanket-stitch from the neck around the head and along the back until you are about 4 cm (1½ in) from the keyring cord.

17 Using small amounts at a time, stuff craft filling into the opening. Use a paintbrush handle to push filling right into the head and tail.

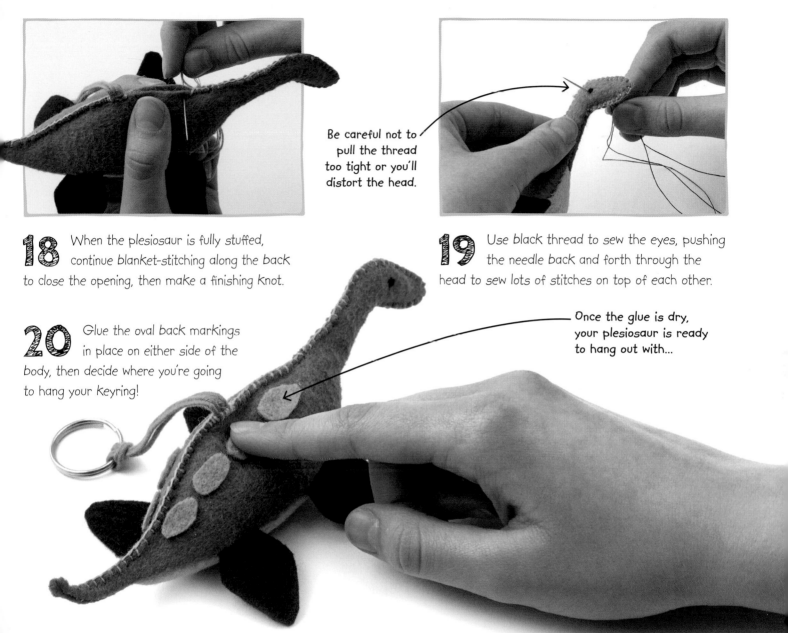

Be careful not to pull the thread too tight or you'll distort the head.

18 When the plesiosaur is fully stuffed, continue blanket-stitching along the back to close the opening, then make a finishing knot.

19 Use black thread to sew the eyes, pushing the needle back and forth through the head to sew lots of stitches on top of each other.

20 Glue the oval back markings in place on either side of the body, then decide where you're going to hang your keyring!

Once the glue is dry, your plesiosaur is ready to hang out with...

ITCHES YOU'LL USE

arting knot
ot your thread at one d so it stays in place. If u can, "hide" the knot the underside or inside your fabric.

Running stitch
Push the needle in and out of the fabric, then pull the thread through. Repeat, keeping the stitches in a straight line.

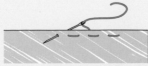

Blanket stitch
Pull the thread up through the fabric, loop it around and push the needle back through next to the stitch. Take the needle through the loop you've just made, then pull the thread tight. Continue stitching, putting your needle through the loop each time before pulling tight.

Finishing knot
Make a stitch but, before pulling it tight, take the needle back through the loop of the stitch. Pull it tight, then repeat once more.

DINO-FEET PEN-POTS

Dinosaurs have left many traces on our planet, including their actual footprints fossilized in rocks. Those footprints tell us a lot about the dinosaurs who lived on Earth millions of years ago, but you can have dinosaurs roaming your desk right now with these *Allosaurus* pen-pots made of papier mâché.

Allosaurus had three strong front toes, plus a small inner toe held off the ground.

Use your "feet" to keep all your pencils, pens, and brushes tidy.

Papier mâché takes a while to dry, so allow time for this project.

Make the "skin" of your dino-feet as smooth or as rough as you like.

MAKE YOUR OWN
DINO-FEET PEN-POTS

Use your measuring skills to create cardboard bases for these pen- or pencil-holders, then use papier mâché to build and sculpt the bases into dino-feet. These steps are for *Allosaurus* feet, but you can model a different dinosaur if you wish.

Time 90 minutes, plus overnight soaking and 7 days drying time

Difficulty Medium

Warning Ask an adult for help with the hot water

WHAT YOU NEED

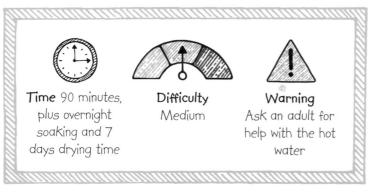

White card

Corrugated card

Wooden spoon

Masking tape

Ruler

Large cardboard tube

Newspaper

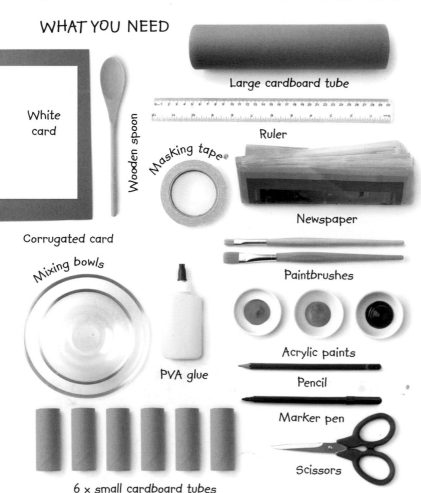

Mixing bowls

PVA glue

Paintbrushes

Acrylic paints

Pencil

Marker pen

Scissors

6 x small cardboard tubes

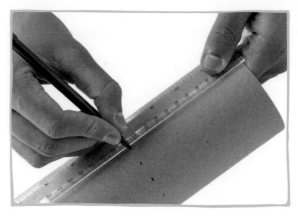

1 Make a series of marks, 10 cm (4 in) from one end, all the way around the large cardboard tube.

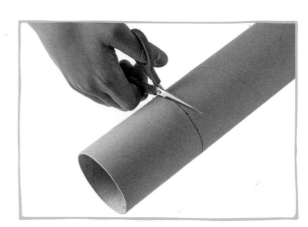

2 Join the marks into a line, then cut along it. If you can't get your scissors into the card, press a pencil through to make a hole. Repeat steps 1–2 at the other end of the tube for the second foot.

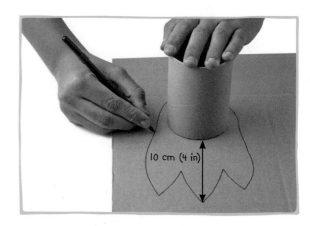
10 cm (4 in)

3 On the corrugated card, draw around a tube. Then draw a foot shape, allowing space around the tube, and about 10 cm (4 in) to the middle toe.

Allosaurus was a fast hunter that ran on two hind feet.

Flipping over the first foot will make your second foot a mirror image of the first.

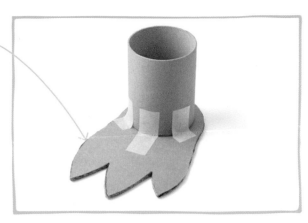

4 Cut out the foot and flip it over to use as a template for the other foot, so you have a pair. Carefully cut out the second foot too.

5 Flip the first foot back over again. Glue the end of a tube and stick it in the position you marked in step 3. Fix it in place with masking tape.

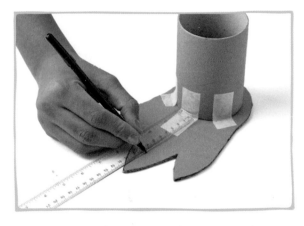

Join up the marks to draw a line parallel with the edge of the card.

6 Measure along the middle toe to a point 6 cm (2½ in) from the base of the tube and make a mark. (This will allow 4 cm [1½ in] for the shaping of the toe when the papier mâché goes on.)

7 Cut one of the small tubes lengthways and lay it flat. Make a series of marks across it 6 cm (2½ in) from one end, and use a ruler to join them up into a line.

You might find it easiest to roll the card round a pencil.

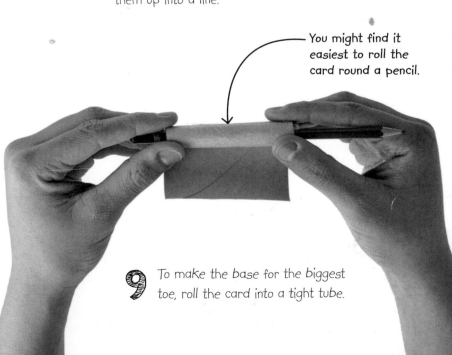

8 Using the line as a guide, cut the card to size and discard the smaller piece into your recycling bin.

9 To make the base for the biggest toe, roll the card into a tight tube.

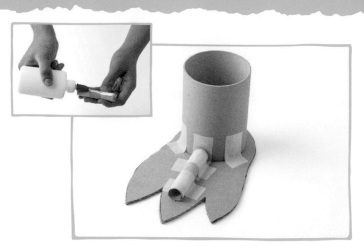

10 Secure the tightly rolled card with masking tape at both ends to make a cylinder about 1.5 cm (½ in) in diameter.

11 Put a line of glue along the tube and stick it in place to form the big middle toe on the top of the foot. Tape it in place.

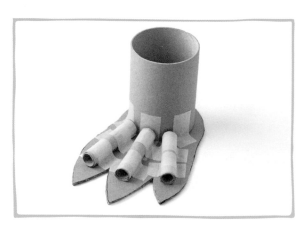

Newspaper is fibrous and will break down easily when soaked in water.

12 Repeat steps 6–11 for the remaining toes, measuring from the tube to 4 cm (1½ in) from the tip of each toe. Then repeat steps 5–12 to make the second foot.

13 Tear the newspaper into strips about 14 cm (5 in) long, then tear the strips into small squares roughly 2 cm x 2 cm (1 in x 1 in). (Torn pieces break down better than straight-cut pieces.)

Soaking softens the paper fibres.

Get stuck in! Mush the mixture with your hands.

14 Put them in a large bowl and cover with boiling water (ask an adult to help you). Carefully stir with a wooden spoon to make sure everything is wet through. Leave overnight to soak.

15 Next morning, squish the pulpy mixture, rubbing it through your fingers to break down the paper fibres. Keep kneeding until your papier mâché mixture has a smooth texture.

Add a dollop of glue about the size of a table-tennis ball.

16 One handful at a time, squeeze the mixture hard to push out as much water as you can. Throw away the water you squeeze out.

17 Put the lumps of squeezed mixture back in the large bowl. Break them up with your hands, then add some PVA glue.

Use your hands to work the glue into the fibrous pulp.

18 Adding more small dollops of glue as necessary, work the mixture thoroughly until it comes together and sticks easily.

19 When ready, the papier mâché will feel like modelling clay. Then wash your hands.

All the tape will be covered up once you have applied the papier mâché.

20 Paint the cardboard base of your dinosaur foot with glue to ensure the papier mâché will stick to it.

21 Using small lumps at a time, start to apply papier mâché to the base. Work along the toes first.

Make the dino skin as smooth or as textured as you like.

22 Continue applying small lumps of papier mâché to shape the foot and work up to the top of the tube.

Try to make the rim of the holder as neat and smooth as you can.

23 Finish covering the first foot, then repeat steps 20–23 for the second foot. Let them dry out (this may take a week). Wash your hands.

24 When the feet are completely dry, paint them inside and out with the base colour you've chosen, and leave to dry.

25 Use a smaller brush and a different colour to paint the skin pattern you want on your dinosaur feet, then leave to dry.

Keep the brush quite dry to make the colours look streaky.

26 To make the dinosaur's claws, paint a piece of white card with streaks of two different brown paints. Leave to dry.

28 Glue each claw in place. Leave to dry, and then fill the pots with your pens, pencils, and paintbrushes.

27 On the back of the card, draw the shape of your dinosaur claws. Cut them out and bend each one around a pencil to give it a curve.

Push firmly to make sure the claws stick well.

STEP UP!

If you want to make a different set of feet, just vary the shape you draw in step 3 and change the shape, number, or size of the claws or hooves you make in step 27. Take a look at some of the tracks below for inspiration...

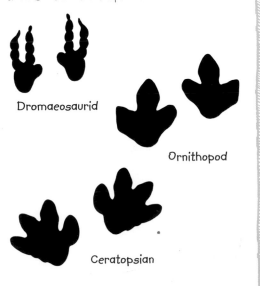

Dromaeosaurid

Ornithopod

Ceratopsian

PREHISTORIC WORLD
MAKING TRACKS

Which dinosaur made which footprint? Sauropods had flat pads, for example, while theropods such as the *Allosaurus* shown here ran on three of their toes and had vicious claws. Fossilized footprints can tell us a lot about which dinosaurs lived in herds, and how fast or slow they might have been. There are even fossil footprints showing signs of broken toes and limping!

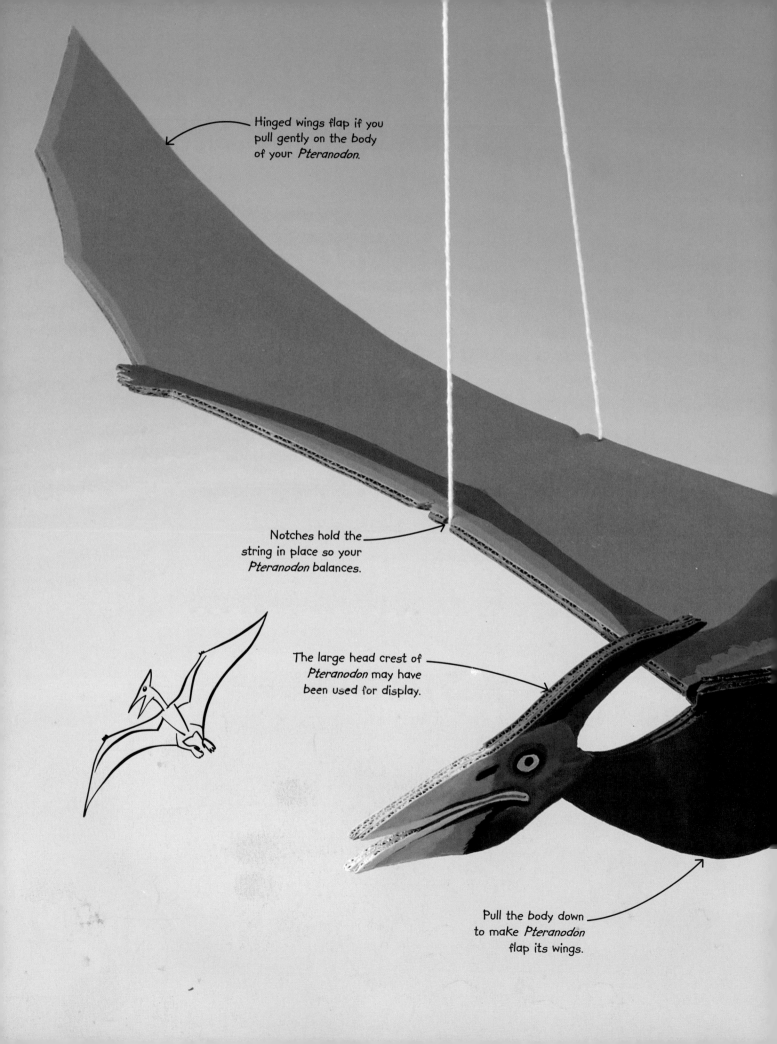

Hinged wings flap if you pull gently on the body of your *Pteranodon*.

Notches hold the string in place so your *Pteranodon* balances.

The large head crest of *Pteranodon* may have been used for display.

Pull the body down to make *Pteranodon* flap its wings.

Pterosaur wings were made of skin stretched between the legs and fingers.

FLYING HIGH
FLAPPING PTERANODON

One of the largest pterosaurs, *Pteranodon* probably soared most of the time and flapped its huge wings only occasionally, but gravity and the clever hinges on this mobile mean you can flap your *Pteranodon's* wings whenever you want!

MAKE YOUR OWN
PTERANODON MOBILE

This clever mobile works with gravity. It hangs naturally at its centre of gravity – the point at which it's balanced and the weight is evenly distributed. If you briefly pull it away from that point, however, the hinged wings will flap until gravity helps it regain its balance.

Time	**Difficulty**	**Warning**
90 minutes, plus drying time	Medium	Ask an adult to cut the dowel for you and hang the mobile up

WHAT YOU NEED

Pencil

Scissors

Paintbrushes

Craft card

Acrylic paints in a variety of colours

PVA glue

2 x 1 m (3 ft) lengths of string

Strong adhesive tape

2 x water bottles

Ruler

Dowel

TEMPLATES

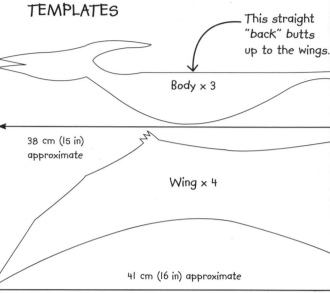

This straight "back" butts up to the wings.

Body x 3

38 cm (15 in) approximate

Wing x 4

41 cm (16 in) approximate

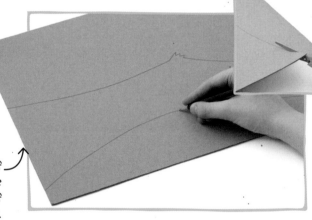

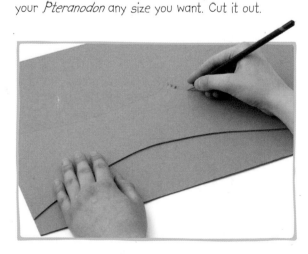

Use the side of the card for the straight edge of the wing.

1 Against the straight edge of the craft card, draw a wing, roughly following the shape above. Use the approximate measurements above, or make your *Pteranodon* any size you want. Cut it out.

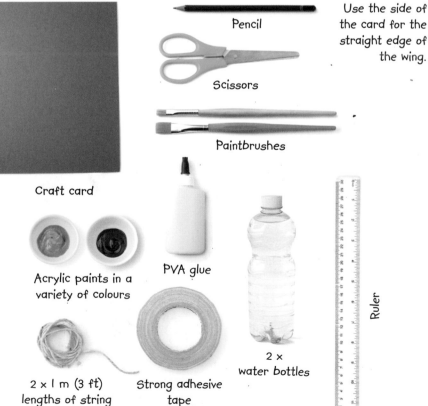

2 Using the cut-out wing as a template, draw around it three more times. Cut them all out so you have four wing pieces in total.

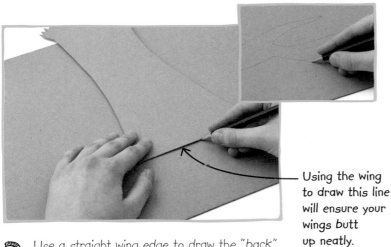

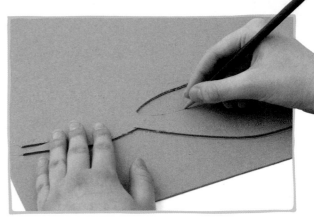

3 Use a straight wing edge to draw the "back" of your *Pteranodon*. Sketch the rest of the body shape around it, roughly following the template.

Using the wing to draw this line will ensure your wings butt up neatly.

4 Cut out the body shape and then use it as a template to draw round twice more. Cut both out, so you have three body pieces in total.

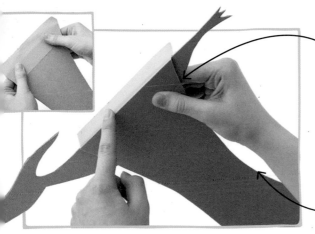

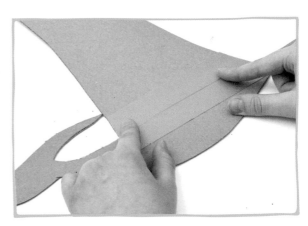

Run the tape along the edges of the card as well as over the flat sides.

5 Stick adhesive tape along the straight edge of one wing piece, line it up with the straight back of one body piece, and tape them together.

The longer curved wing side should be nearest the tail end of the body.

6 Lift the wing up and lay it flat above the body. Secure it with another strip of adhesive tape, then fold it down below the body again.

The tape creates hinges that allow the wings to flap.

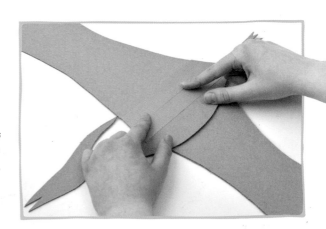

7 Repeat step 5 to stick a wing piece on the other side of the body. Wrap the tape over both the body and the other wing.

8 Repeat step 6 for the second wing, so you have a wing on each side of the body, and tape on the top and underside of each wing.

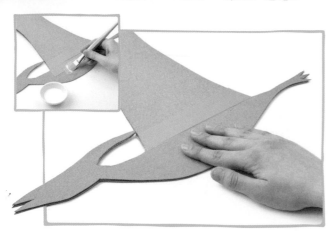

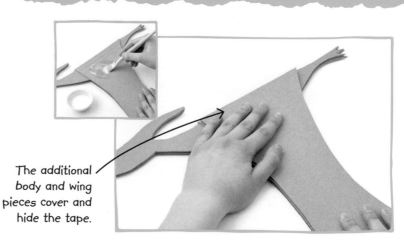

The additional body and wing pieces cover and hide the tape.

9 Lift the wings out of the way and brush glue all over one side of the body. Stick a second body piece down onto it. Turn over and repeat on the other side with the remaining body piece.

10 Fold both wings down. Brush a wing with glue and stick one of the remaining wing pieces onto it. Repeat on the other side, so each wing has two layers.

The centre of gravity is where the *Pteranodon* is balanced.

11 To find the balancing points, lay your *Pteranodon* across the top of two water bottles, moving them in or out until the *Pteranodon* balances and the wings are horizontal.

12 Mark the position of the bottles, and draw a line across the wing through each mark. Loop the string under each wing along the lines, and lift to check that the *Pteranodon* hangs level.

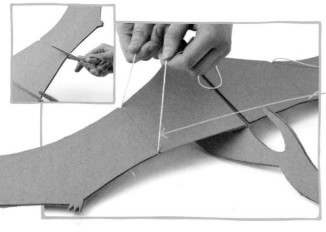

Pteranodon will hang level because its weight is evenly distributed across the strings.

13 If it doesn't hang level, repeat steps 11–12 to adjust the line positions, then cut a notch at both ends of each line to hold the string in place.

14 Paint the wings all over with mid-brown and the body and tail (but not the head) with darker brown. Leave to dry.

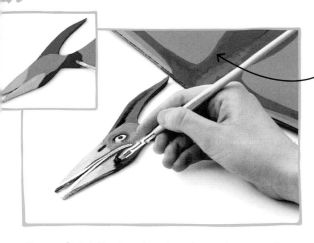

Paint both top and underside of the wings, as you'll see both sides when the wings flap.

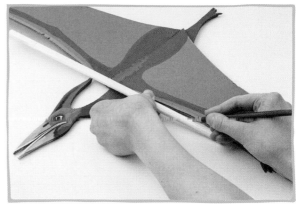

15 Paint the head and neck as shown, and a dark-brown outline of the body and "arms" on the wings. Once dry, add details on the head.

16 On the dowel, mark the wingspan from notch to notch. Add 5 cm (2 in) at either end, and ask an adult to cut it to length for you.

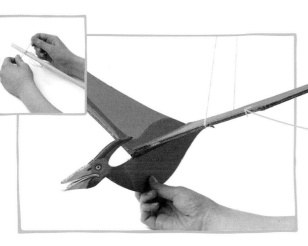

Pteranodon had a wingspan of 7–9 m (23–30 ft).

17 Tie the two loops of string to the dowel, 5 cm (2 in) from each end. Fit the wings through the loops and the string in the notches.

Slide the knots if you need to make any last-minute adjustments for balance.

Your *Pteronodon* is balanced at its centre of gravity – until you pull it, that is!

PREHISTORIC WORLD
WINGED REPTILES

Pterosaurs first took to the skies in the late Triassic Period and were the size of crows, with short necks, toothed jaws, and very long tails. By the late Cretaceous, they had developed toothless, beak-like jaws, the long necks and short tails that made them better fliers, and occasionally colossal proportions – *Quetzalcoatlus*, for example, had the wingspan of a small aeroplane (10 m/33 ft).

Pteronodon could snatch fish while it soared over the waves.

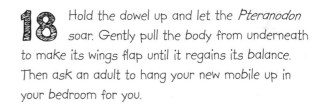

18 Hold the dowel up and let the *Pteranodon* soar. Gently pull the body from underneath to make its wings flap until it regains its balance. Then ask an adult to hang your new mobile up in your bedroom for you.

A SURPRISE DINO-ROAR
POP-UP DINOSAUR CARD

What *better* dinosaur to deliver a pop-up dino-roar than *Parasaurolophus*? The distinctive tube-like bony crest on its head is thought to have worked like a trumpet that amplified its loud, booming calls. When you open the card, the hinged sections of the interlocking shapes let the *Parasaurolophus* pop up.

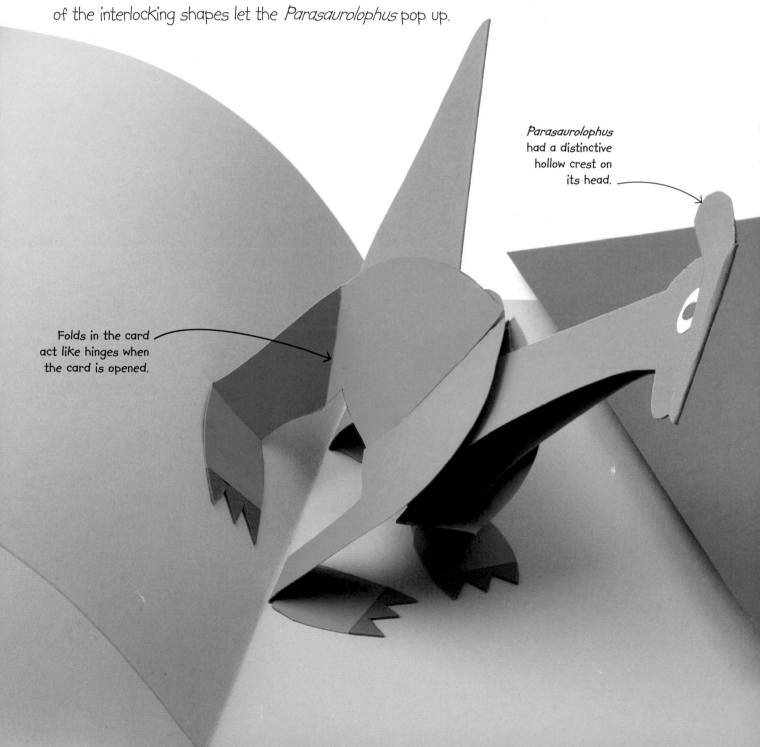

Parasaurolophus had a distinctive hollow crest on its head.

Folds in the card act like hinges when the card is opened.

Flat, 2D card becomes a 3D shape when the card is opened.

The dinosaur is fixed to the card by its feet.

MAKE YOUR OWN
POP-UP DINOSAUR CARD

These shapes slot together cleverly to make a *Parasaurolophus* that pops up when you open the card. The folds in the legs act as hinges that turn the interlocking 2D body shapes into a 3D dinosaur.

Time
45 minutes

Difficulty
Medium

WHAT YOU NEED

White paper

Coloured card

Pencil

Rubber

Set square

Ruler

Marker pen

PVA glue

Scissors

TEMPLATES

Tail
Cut x 1

Tab

Head
Cut x 1

Tab

Body
Cut x 1 to the black outline and x 1 to the red outline

Fold lines

Crest
Cut x 1

Neck
Cut x 1

Tab

Left foot
Cut x 2

Right foot
Cut x 2

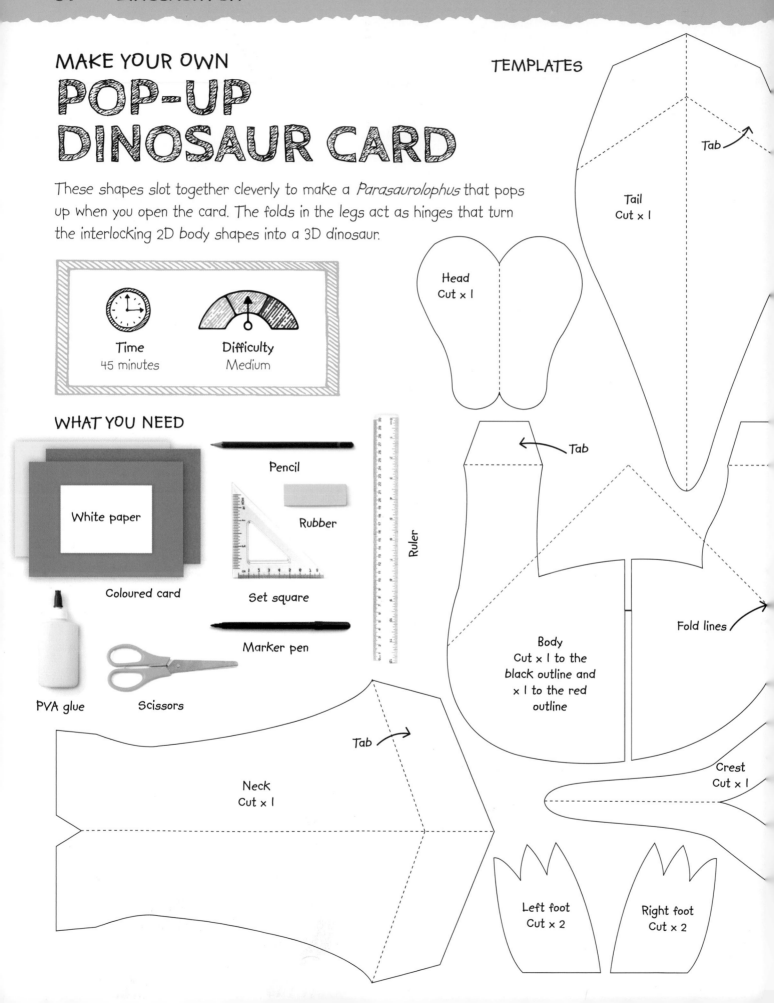

1 First, make your card. Fold a 21 cm x 30 cm (8¼ in x 11¾ in) sheet of coloured card in half, then unfold it and mark the fold line in pencil.

2 Measure the halfway point along the fold line and use a set square to draw an intersecting line at 90° to it.

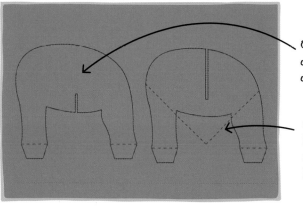

One copy has only the black outline: Body A.

One copy has the red marks too: Body B.

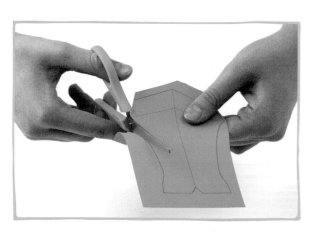

3 Copy the body template opposite, drawing two copies of it on another piece of coloured card. On one copy, follow the black marks only; on the other, transfer the red marks as shown.

4 Copy all the other templates too, except the feet. Use different-coloured card for the crest piece (we've used yellow, but use whatever colour you like). Carefully cut out all the pieces.

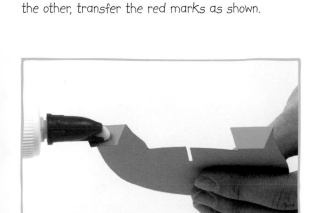

Position the slot in Body A along the intersecting line.

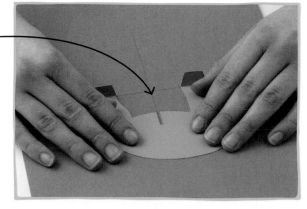

5 On the Body A piece, fold along the tabs indicated by the dotted lines. Put a dab of glue on the underside of each tab.

6 Line up the tab folds of Body A with the fold line on the card, and the slot in Body A with the intersecting line you drew at 90°.

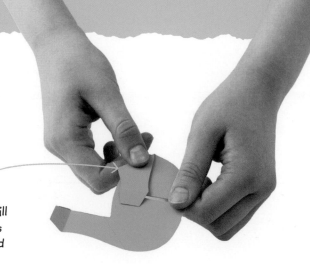

These folds will act as hinges when the card is opened.

7 Bring the orange card up to the tabs and stick them to it. Fold the card over completely and press to stick the tabs down firmly.

8 Crease both legs of Body B along the red diagonal fold lines marked on the template. Fold the feet tabs in the same direction.

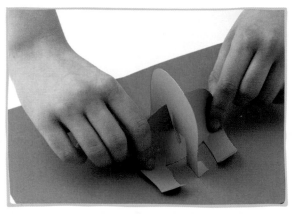

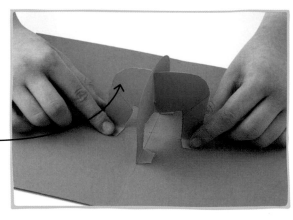

Note that both Body A and B are smaller on one side of the slot than the other.

9 Open the orange card. Slide Body B carefully under Body A, then unfold its legs and ease the slot on Body B up into the slot on Body A.

10 Line up the two feet tabs of Body B with the intersecting line. Fold the orange card gently to check the legs are bending correctly.

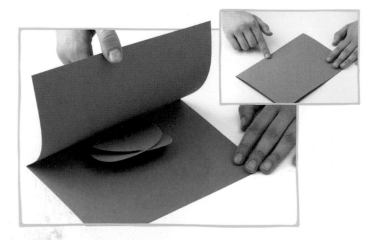

11 Unfold the card, add a drop of glue to the two tabs on Body B, then re-fold the card and press firmly to stick the Body B tabs to it.

12 Next, fold the neck piece firmly in half along the dotted line across the middle of the template.

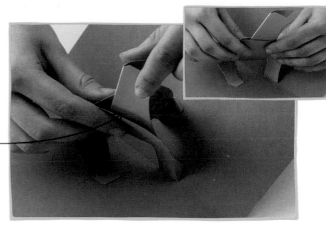

Stick the neck tabs to the bigger sides of the two body pieces.

13 Open out again and fold back the end with the dotted lines marked for the tabs. Re-fold in half and press firmly.

14 Apply glue to the tabs of the neck. Position it, folded side upwards, between Body A and Body B. Press firmly to glue in place.

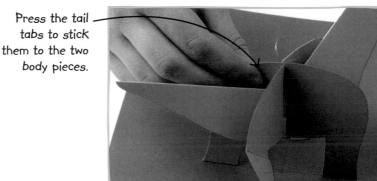

Press the tail tabs to stick them to the two body pieces.

15 Fold the tail piece in half at the dotted line along the centre of the template. Then open out and fold one end back along the dotted tab line. Re-fold in half and press firmly.

16 Glue the folded tabs on the tail and attach between Body A and Body B on the opposite side to the neck, folded side upwards.

17 Carefully fold the orange card and press firmly to make sure everything is stuck together. Then reopen the card and rub out the pencil lines.

Strong hind legs meant *Parasaurolophus* could probably rear up to feed on taller trees.

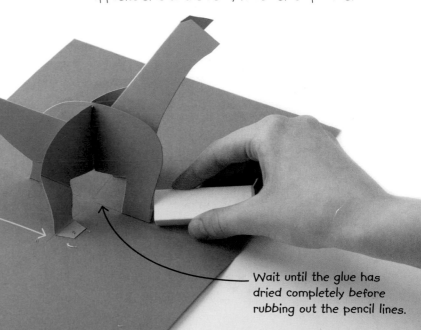

Wait until the glue has dried completely before rubbing out the pencil lines.

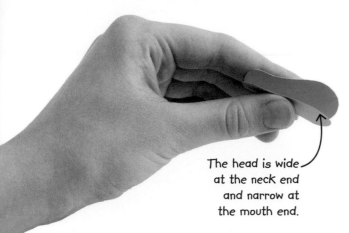

The head is wide at the neck end and narrow at the mouth end.

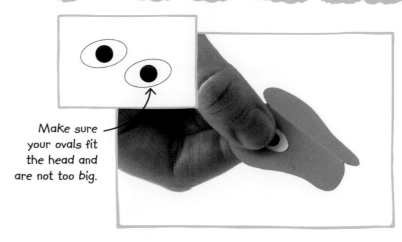

Make sure your ovals fit the head and are not too big.

18 Fold the head piece in half and press the crease down firmly. Then turn it over so the fold is upwards.

19 To make eyes, draw two ovals on white paper. Draw black circles with a marker pen for pupils. Cut out the ovals and glue one on each side of the wide part of the head.

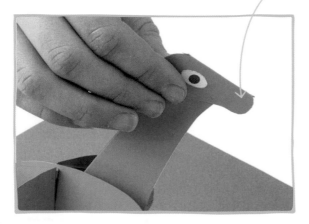

A tough, sharp beak helped *Parasaurolophus* crop leaves to eat.

Put the widest part of the crest at the back of the head.

20 Apply glue to the inside of the head and attach it to the top of the neck. Squeeze firmly until the glue holds the head in place.

21 Fold the yellow crest along the dotted line. Glue it on top of the head, as shown, and press firmly to stick the pieces together.

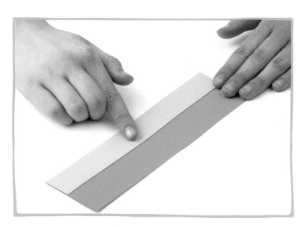

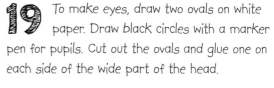

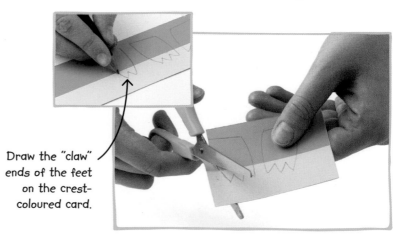

Draw the "claw" ends of the feet on the crest-coloured card.

22 For the feet, cut a strip of card 15 cm x 5 cm (6 in x 2 in) in the main colour and one half as wide in the crest colour. Glue together.

23 Copy each foot template twice onto the strip, positioning the "claws" on the crest-coloured strip. Cut out the four feet.

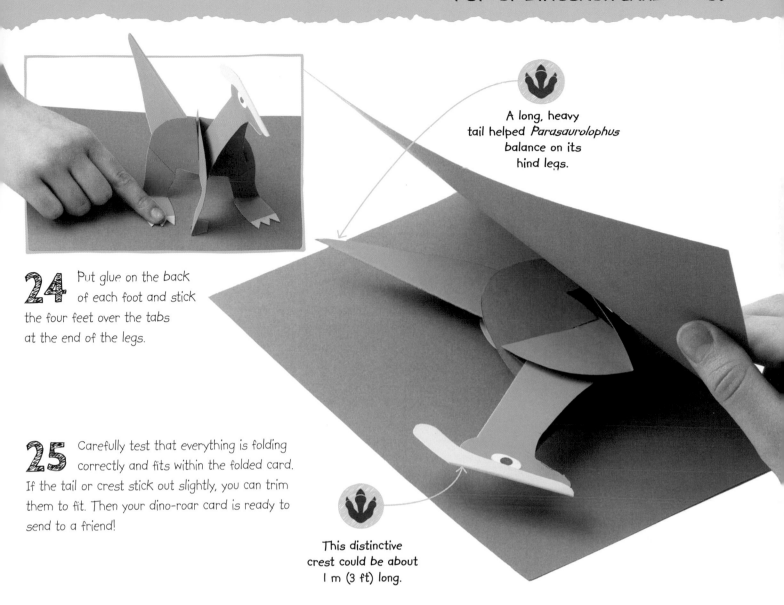

A long, heavy
tail helped *Parasaurolophus*
balance on its
hind legs.

24 Put glue on the back
of each foot and stick
the four feet over the tabs
at the end of the legs.

25 Carefully test that everything is folding
correctly and fits within the folded card.
If the tail or crest stick out slightly, you can trim
them to fit. Then your dino-roar card is ready to
send to a friend!

This distinctive
crest could be about
1 m (3 ft) long.

PREHISTORIC WORLD
CRESTS AND CALLS

Parasaurolophus had the longest
crest of any known dinosaur, but many
fellow hadrosaurs also had hollow crests.
These may have been used like a trumpet,
to make their calls louder, with the length
of the crest affecting the pitch. The
Parasaurolophus crest started growing
much earlier in life compared to its close
cousins, helping the crest reach such
unusual proportions.

Inside the crest
was an airway
connecting the
animal's throat
to its nostrils.

DINO-EGG BATH BOMBS

When these eggs hit the water, a chemical reaction takes place that releases fizzy bubbles of carbon dioxide gas. As the bath bombs break up, the other ingredients of your egg are released – including a hidden baby dinosaur!

The fizzing is carbon dioxide being released – that's what causes the bubbles in the bath wate

The bath bomb dissolves to "hatch" a baby dinosaur.

These eggs are delicate, so handle them just like a real egg.

MAKE YOUR OWN
DINO-EGG BATH BOMBS

These eggs fizz due to an acid-base reaction: the citric acid reacts with a base of bicarbonate of soda to produce fizzy bubbles. Add an essential oil that you like the smell of, such as lemon or lavender, and a few drops of food colouring to give your bath bombs some colour.

1 Mix the citric acid, cornflour, and bicarbonate of soda together in a large bowl.

Time 30 minutes, plus 3 days drying time

Difficulty Easy

WHAT YOU NEED

50 g (2 oz) citric acid

25 g (1 oz) cornflour

Large bowl

Essential oil

100 g (3¾ oz) bicarbonate of soda

Tablespoon

Teaspoon

Food colouring

2 tablespoons of olive oil

Egg moulds

Spray bottle of water

Small bowl

Small dinosaur toys

Whisk

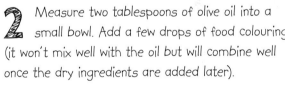

Choose food colouring to suit the colour you want for your bath bomb.

2 Measure two tablespoons of olive oil into a small bowl. Add a few drops of food colouring (it won't mix well with the oil but will combine well once the dry ingredients are added later).

Be careful – you only need a few drops of essential oil.

3 Add a few drops of an essential oil to make your bath eggs smell nice. Mix all the liquid ingredients together with your spoon.

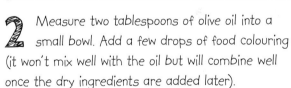
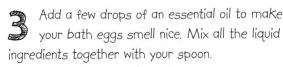

As the liquid is added, the colour of the mixture gets darker and darker.

4 Add a few drops of the oil mixture into the large bowl with the dry ingredients in it, and mix them together with a whisk.

5 Continue adding small amounts of the oil mixture, a little bit at a time, and whisking in between additions.

The chemicals in this mixture will react with the bath water to release fizzy carbon dioxide bubbles.

6 Once you have finished adding the oil mixture, the ingredients in the bowl should be coloured and crumbly.

7 Gently spray the mix with a fine mist spray – carefully add just a little water at a time or it will make the mixture start to fizz.

The mixture should feel damp and a bit sticky, like wet sand.

Push the mixture firmly into the mould.

8 Work the mixture together with your hands – it should just be able to stick together but still be quite crumbly.

9 Pack one half of your egg mould with the mixture (the oil in the mixture should prevent it from sticking to the mould).

Press hard to push the dinosaur toy up into the packed mixture.

10 Push your little dinosaur toy halfway down into the mixture inside the mould. Then pack the other half of the egg mould with mixture.

11 Line up the two halves of the mould, ready to push them together with the dinosaur hidden inside.

12 Push firmly to squeeze the two halves together, clean off the outside of the mould, and then leave to set overnight.

13 Carefully remove the top half of the mould and ease the egg bomb out of the other half. Leave it to set for 1–2 days in a dry place, then pop it into your next bath and "hatch" your own baby dino.

Be very gentle, as the bath bomb might still be a bit crumbly.

PREHISTORIC WORLD
SHAPES AND SIZES

Dinosaur eggs came in various shapes and sizes. Those of an oviraptorid were long and oval, while sauropod eggs were almost spherical. Some would fit in the palm of your hand, but others were the size of a basketball – or even larger. Big dinosaurs didn't necessarily lay big eggs, however; the baby dinosaurs just grew very fast once hatched.

Oviraptorid eggs were laid in a spiral pattern in the nest.

GIANT DINOSAUR EGG

All dinosaurs laid eggs, just like their closest living relatives, birds and crocodiles. And just like hens' eggs, although up to seven times bigger, some dinosaur eggs had hard, chalky shells. Make this giant dinosaur egg out of papier mâché, and then try a "hatched" one – which means there'll be a baby dinosaur loose somewhere...!

You could sit your egg on a nest of twigs or leaves.

MAKE YOUR OWN
GIANT DINOSAUR EGG

To make this giant dinosaur egg, you'll need to use an inflated balloon as a model and then cover it in papier mâché. You'll need a little bit of patience too, as you need to leave the egg to dry overnight, three times in total.

Time 3 hours, plus 3 nights' drying time

Difficulty Easy

WHAT YOU NEED

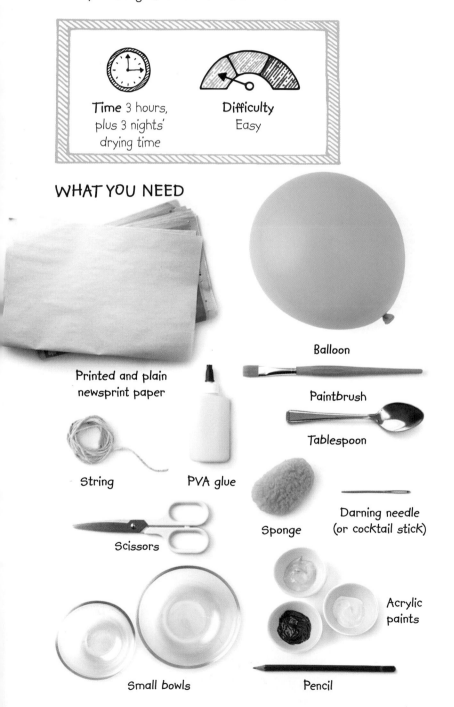

Printed and plain newsprint paper

Balloon

Paintbrush

Tablespoon

String   PVA glue

Scissors

Sponge

Darning needle (or cocktail stick)

Acrylic paints

Small bowls   Pencil

1 Tear the printed newspaper into about 4 cm (1½ in) squares. You want torn, rough edges, as they will blend together well for the papier mâché.

2 Blow up your balloon. In a small bowl, mix equal amounts of glue and water. (You'll need to top up your glue solution every so often; just remember to mix equal amounts of glue and water.)

3 Paint a section of balloon with glue, stick on a layer of overlapping paper squares, and smooth it down with more glue. Then move on to another bit.

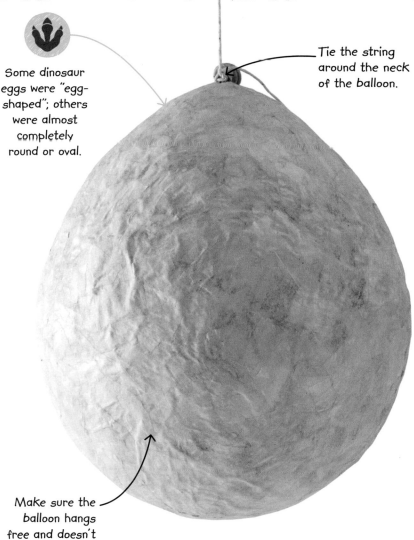

Some dinosaur eggs were "egg-shaped"; others were almost completely round or oval.

Tie the string around the neck of the balloon.

4 Glue the squares up as close as you can to the neck of the balloon. Continue until the balloon is completely covered in newspaper and glue.

5 Repeat step 1, but this time tearing up the plain newspaper into squares. Remember, you want rough edges rather than straight ones.

Make sure the balloon hangs free and doesn't touch anything.

7 Hang the balloon up overnight, to let the papier mâché dry fully. Then repeat steps 3–7, so the balloon ends up covered with four layers of paper – printed, plain, printed, plain.

Using the plain paper helps you see which areas you have already done and which ones you haven't.

6 Using the plain squares, repeat steps 3–4. As before, overlap the edges and take the layer right up to the neck of the balloon.

8 Once the papier mâché has dried completely, poke a darning needle or cocktail stick through the gap near the neck to pop the balloon.

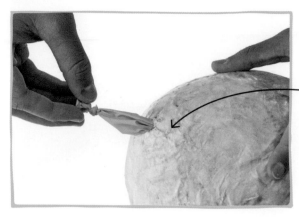

Take care not to damage the hole when you pull the balloon out.

9 After the balloon has popped and the air has seeped out, carefully pull the deflated balloon through the hole in the papier mâché.

10 To seal the hole, repeat the process of gluing layers of newspaper over that small section, starting with a layer of printed paper squares.

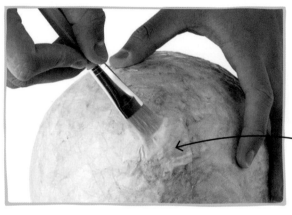

The papier mâché is quite robust, but do brush gently.

Once you've finished, you shouldn't be able to see where the hole had been.

11 Alternate printed/plain newspaper as before in four layers, then leave overnight to dry.

12 Next, paint the egg with a coat of beige paint. Leave to dry.

Work in sections so your colours stay separate and speckled.

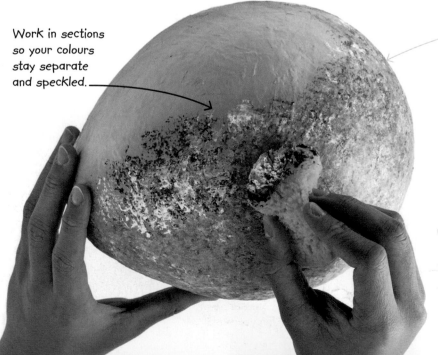

Dinosaur egg shells could be bumpy or smooth, and may have had different colours and patterns.

13 Finally, dip a sponge into white paint and gently dab it onto a section of egg. Repeat with the beige and the dark-brown paint, to speckle the egg all over. Leave to dry.

GET CRACKING

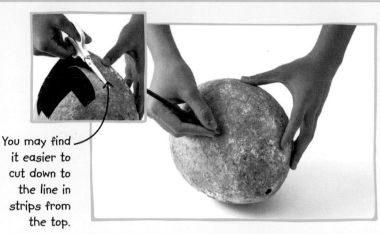

You may find it easier to cut down to the line in strips from the top.

1 To make an egg that's "cracked open", follow steps 1–9 as outlined, but don't close up the hole at the neck of the balloon. Instead, draw a jagged line to mark where your egg will "crack".

2 Insert the tip of a pair of scissors into the hole and carefully cut down to the line you have marked. Cut away the top of the egg by cutting along the jagged line you've drawn.

3 Paint the inside of your egg with two coats of white paint, leaving it to dry between each coat. You'll need to repeat steps 1–3 if you want to make two "halves".

To cover up the newsprint, you'll need at least two coats of paint.

PREHISTORIC WORLD
IN THE NEST

Dinosaurs often laid large clutches of eggs, and there have been many fossilized nest sites found – some even have fossilized adult dinosaurs sitting on them. The biggest dinosaurs didn't sit on their eggs, incubating them in pits filled with earth and warm, rotting leaves instead. This egg was fossilized just as the baby dinosaur was about to hatch. In the same way that modern birds do, the baby dinosaur was "tucking", ready to push its way out of its shell.

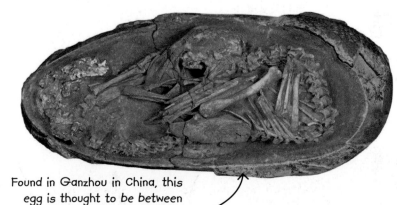

Found in Ganzhou in China, this egg is thought to be between 71 and 66 million years old.

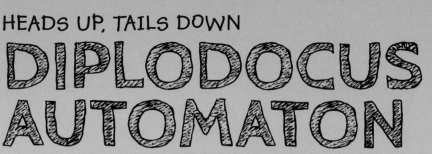

HEADS UP, TAILS DOWN
DIPLODOCUS AUTOMATON

With its amazingly long neck and even longer tail, *Diplodocus* is the perfect dinosaur for this clever machine. This project will awaken your inner engineer as you create the model's moving parts – which are all hidden inside that green box!

Diplodocus fossil bones suggest that it was an amazing 27 m (88 ft) long from nose to tail.

The head drops down as the tail moves up – to munch on some leaves, or take a drink, perhaps?

Inside the box is a secret machine – one that you can build yourself.

The tail and head move elegantly up and down without you touching them – but how?

Turn the handle and see what happens...

MAKE YOUR OWN
DIPLODOCUS AUTOMATON

For this project, you make a box, a model to sit on top of it, and a machine to go inside it. Your machine uses smooth cams, which are rotating shapes on a camshaft, to move pistons up and down. The automaton templates are half-size; the grid method on page 17 can help you scale them up.

WHAT YOU NEED

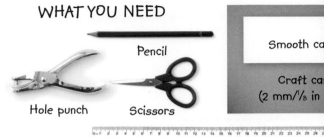

Pencil

Hole punch   Scissors

Smooth car

Craft care
(2 mm/⅛ in t

Ruler

Masking tape

4 × lengths of dowel: 1 × 30 cm (12 in)
2 × 15 cm (6 in), 1 × 5 cm (2 in)

Paper fasteners

Paintbrushes   2 × 10 cm (4 in)
pieces of string

Compass

Time 2½ hours, plus drying time

Difficulty Hard

2 × metal washers
(with central holes wide
enough for the dowel)

Acrylic paints in a
variety of colours

PVA glue

Strong adhe
tape

AUTOMATON TEMPLATES

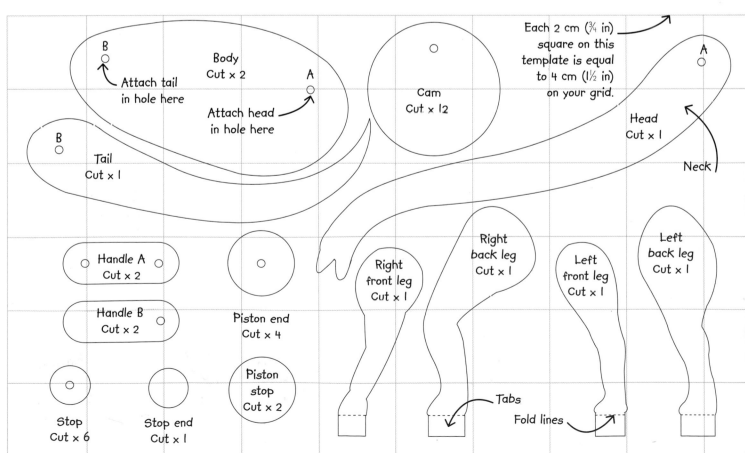

B
Attach tail
in hole here

Body
Cut × 2

A
Attach head
in hole here

B
Tail
Cut × 1

Cam
Cut × 12

Each 2 cm (¾ in) square on this template is equal to 4 cm (1½ in) on your grid.

A

Head
Cut × 1

Neck

Handle A
Cut × 2

Handle B
Cut × 2

Piston end
Cut × 4

Right
front leg
Cut × 1

Right
back leg
Cut × 1

Left
front leg
Cut × 1

Left
back leg
Cut × 1

Stop
Cut × 6

Stop end
Cut × 1

Piston
stop
Cut × 2

Tabs   Fold lines

BOX TEMPLATES

| Side piece A Cut x 2 (25 cm x 14 cm/ 10 in x 5½ in) | Side piece B Cut x 2 (14 cm x 17 cm/5½ in x 6¾ in) | Centre piece Cut x 1 (25 cm x 17 cm/ 10 in x 6¾ in) | Main piece Cut x 1 (53 cm x 48 cm/ 21 in x 19 in) |

End panels on the main piece are the same size as side piece B.

Fold lines

Side panels on the main piece are the same size as side piece A.

1 Measure out the shapes of all the box pieces onto craft card, as shown, and cut them all out.

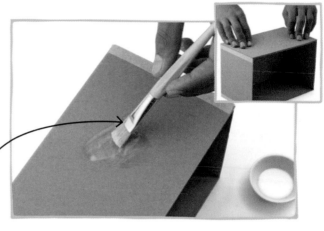

Glue a second piece to each side to make it double-thickness.

2 Score and fold the four fold lines on the main piece to make a box that's open on one side, and secure all the joins with masking tape.

3 Apply glue to one side of the box and stick on a matching side piece. Repeat for the other three sides and centre piece. Leave to dry.

Where the two diagonal lines cross is the centre point of the shape.

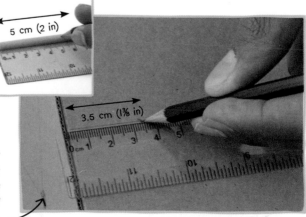

5 cm (2 in)

3.5 cm (1⅜ in)

Make your marks in line with the holes on the sides of the box.

4 At the centre points on both of the two small sides of the box, push a pencil through to make a hole. Insert the 30 cm (12 in) dowel to check that it moves freely.

5 On the 30 cm (12 in) dowel, mark off 5 cm (2 in) from one end and 7 cm (2¾ in) from the other. Draw a rule across a long side of the box, in line with the holes, and mark off 3.5 cm (1⅜ in) from both ends.

6 Make a hole with a pencil at each of the two marks you made on the box in step 5. Check that a dowel can move freely through the holes.

A compass radius of 4 cm (1½ in) will give your circle a diameter of 8 cm (3 in).

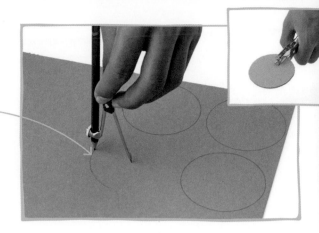

7 Set your compass to a radius of 4 cm (1½ in) and draw the 12 cam circles. Punch holes where indicated on the template.

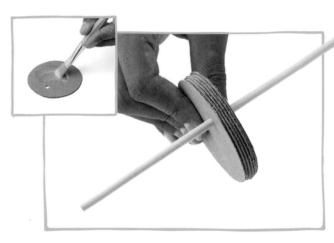

8 Brush glue onto six cam pieces and stack them together. Use the dowel to line up the holes, then remove it. Repeat for the other six cams.

The smooth surface will ensure the parts move freely, with no friction.

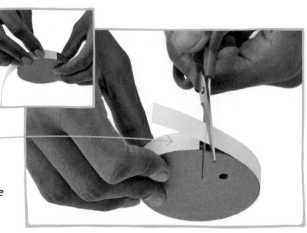

9 Cut two strips of smooth card, 26 cm x 1.5 cm (10 in x ⅝ in). Glue a strip around the rim of each cam stack, and trim the excess.

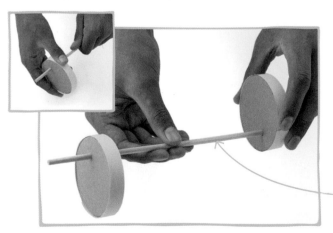

10 Position a cam on the dowel, over one of the marks you made in step 5, and glue it in place. Then glue the other cam over the other mark, fixing it the opposite way up.

Insert the long end through the left hole first, and then the shorter end on the right.

This dowel will become a camshaft that turns the cams when you move the handle.

11 Next, insert the camshaft with the cams attached into the two holes on the sides of the box. Ensure it moves freely in the holes.

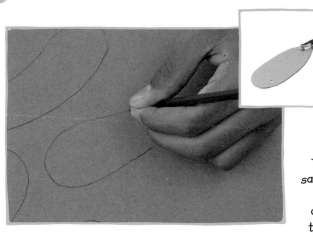

The squares are sandwiched by the body pieces and create space for the head and tail to move freely.

12 Copy all the remaining template pieces onto craft card (using the grid method on page 17). Cut them out and punch holes where marked on the template.

13 Cut two squares of card 4 cm by 4 cm (1½ in by 1½ in). Glue them together, then glue them *between* the two body pieces, lining up the body pieces and their holes.

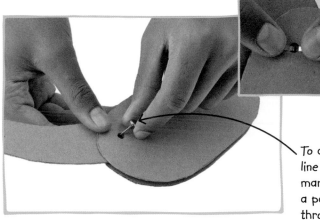

To attach the neck, line up the holes marked A and push a paper fastener through them.

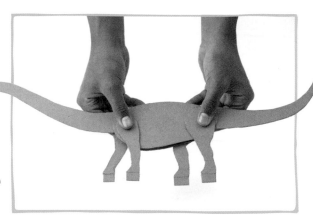

14 Slide the neck between the body pieces and secure it in place with a paper fastener. Repeat for the tail with the holes marked B.

15 Glue the front and back legs in position, as shown. Hold until the glue sets, then bend the leg tabs in towards the body.

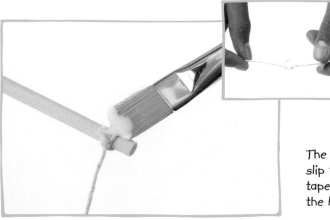

The string won't slip through the tape because of the knot in it.

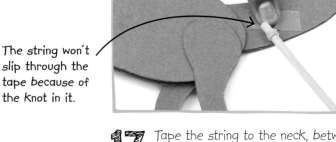

16 Tie a piece of string to one end of a 15 cm (6 in) dowel, and glue it in place. Then make a knot in the string 2 cm (¾ in) away from the dowel.

17 Tape the string to the neck, between the knot and the dowel. Repeat steps 16–17 to fix the other 15 cm (6 in) dowel to the tail.

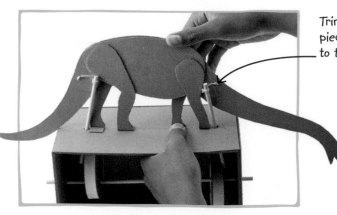

Trim the string pieces close to the knots.

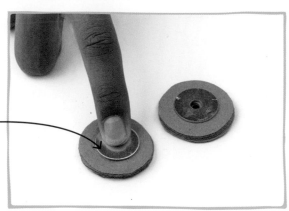

Glue a washer to the top of each piston stack to add extra weight.

18 Slide the dowels into the two holes on the top of the box and glue the foot tabs into position, as shown. Hold until the glue has set.

19 Glue together three piston ends (with their holes in line) and a piston stop, then glue a washer over the hole. Repeat to make a second stack.

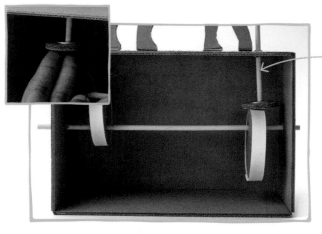

The dowels act as pistons, which move up and down as the cams rotate.

20 Put glue in the hole of a piston stack and push the head dowel into it, then repeat to fix the other piston stack to the tail dowel.

21 Glue three stops and a stop end together. Put glue in the central hole and push it onto the camshaft end outside the box below the head.

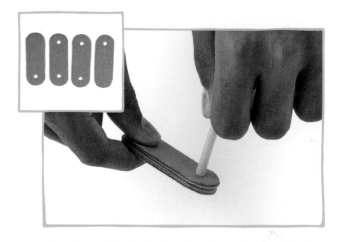

Glue the stops onto the camshaft below the tail and as close to the box as possible.

22 With the holes aligned as shown, glue the handle pieces in a stack. Glue the 5 cm (2 in) dowel into the hole on one side.

23 Stick the remaining stops together, then glue them onto the camshaft. Glue the end of the camshaft into the other side of the handle.

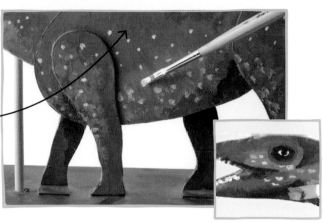

Add small patches of green too if you want.

24 Paint the box green, criss-crossing your strokes and making the paint thicker and thinner in places, for a dappled effect.

25 Paint the *Diplodocus* a mid-brown, then dapple on patches of paler brown, and dot white spots all over the underside. Finally, add details such as eyes, and shading around the head.

As the pistons move, they push the tail and head up and down.

The head moves down when the tail moves up, because of the position of the cams on the camshaft.

Watch the pistons move up and down as the cams rotate.

26 Gently turn the handle to rotate the camshaft and make the head and tail of your *Diplodocus* move gracefully up and down.

PREHISTORIC WORLD
MOBILE NECKS

Plant-eating sauropods such as *Diplodocus* had astonishingly long necks, but the bones within them were full of air cavities that made them light. It used its long neck to sweep a wide area of ground so it could more efficiently eat without moving its large body. *Diplodocus* didn't need to chew leaves, but swallowed them whole, and they passed down that long neck straight into its stomach.

The long neck was supported by at least 15 vertebrae.

The whip-like tail may have been used for defence.

The head was small in relation to the body – with a comparably small brain inside.

TYRANNOSAURUS MASK

Want to be a *Tyrannosaurus* – one of the most powerful land predators that has ever lived on Earth? *Tyrannosaurus* may have roamed the planet for about 2 million years, and its massive size, strong legs and bone-crushing teeth made it a successful hunter. Make this fantastic mask and start practising your roar!

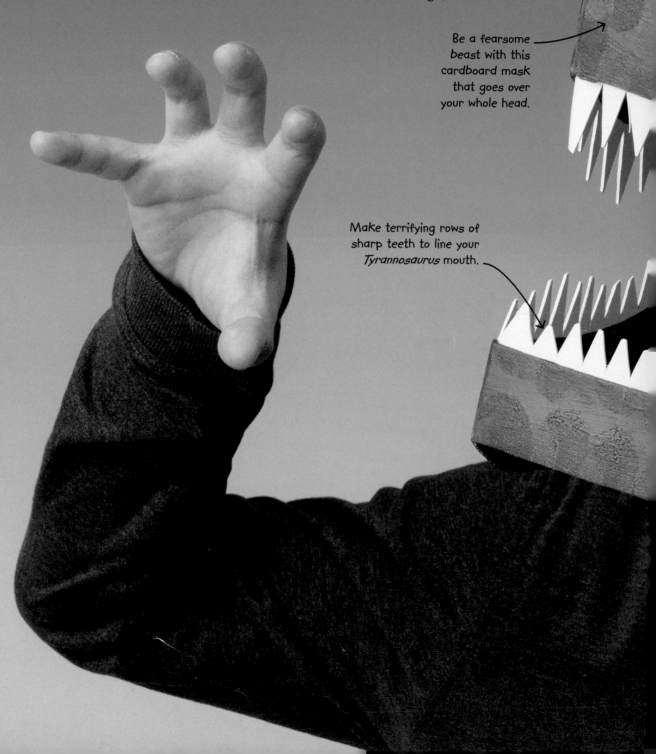

Be a fearsome beast with this cardboard mask that goes over your whole head.

Make terrifying rows of sharp teeth to line your *Tyrannosaurus* mouth.

Use homemade stamps to create the skin patterns on your *Tyrannosaurus* head.

Tyrannosaurus jaws could crush bone. Fossils of their dung have been found full of bone fragments.

MAKE YOUR OWN
TYRANNOSAURUS MASK

You'll need a large piece of card for the main piece – craft card or a large cardboard box is fine. Before you start, it's a good idea to look at the template and read the steps through so you understand how the different 2D shapes all join up to make the 3D mask.

WHAT YOU NEED

Pencil

Marker pen

Paintbrush

White card

Craft card

Washing-up sponge

Scissors

PVA glue

Acrylic paints

Masking tape

Ruler

Time 2 hours, plus drying time

Difficulty Hard

TEMPLATES

You can draw the curved bits freehand, but for the straight lines follow the measurements below.

10 cm (4 in)

3.5 cm (1⅜ in)

Chin
Cut x 1

This edge forms the lower side of the mouth.

3.5 cm (1⅜ in)

Edge C

Lower jaw
Cut x 2

7.5 cm (3 in)

20.5 cm (8⅛ in)

9.5 cm (3¾ in)

155°

155°

6.5 cm (2½ in)

130°

Fold

135°

Upper jaw
Cut x 2

15.5 cm (6⅛ in)

140°

Point A

5 cm (2 in)

130°

Glue area for attaching lower jaw

Fold

95°

This edge forms the upper side of the mouth.

Main piece
Cut x 1

5 cm (2 in)

3.5 cm (1⅜ in)

10 cm (4 in)

5 cm (2 in)

6.5 cm (2½ in)

20.5 cm (8⅛ in)

7.5 cm (3 in)

9.5 cm (3¾ in)

15.5 cm (6⅛ in)

Point B

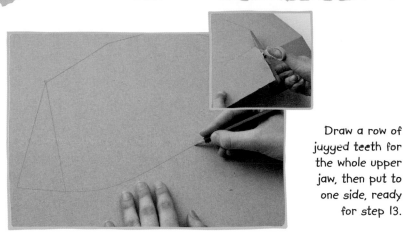

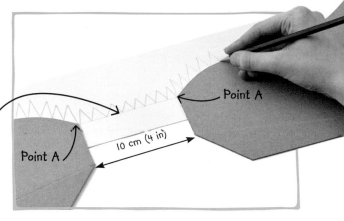

Draw a row of jagged teeth for the whole upper jaw, then put to one side, ready for step 13.

Point A

Point A

10 cm (4 in)

1 Copy the template opposite to draw an upper jaw piece onto craft card. Cut it out and draw round it for the second upper jaw. Cut that out too.

2 Put the pieces upside-down, facing each other, on white card. Draw a line between the point As, then draw jagged teeth along the whole jawline.

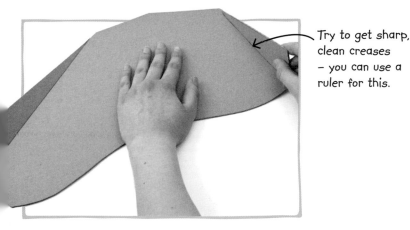

Try to get sharp, clean creases – you can use a ruler for this.

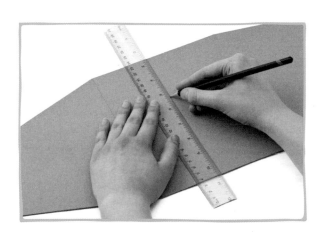

3 Fold the upper jaw pieces along the fold lines indicated. Put a ruler on a fold line, lift the card up against it, and press along the underside edge.

4 Carefully following the measurements on the template, copy and cut out the main piece. Mark all the fold lines shown.

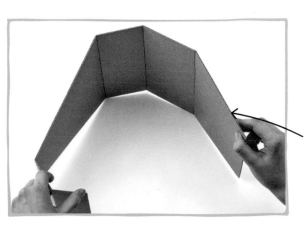

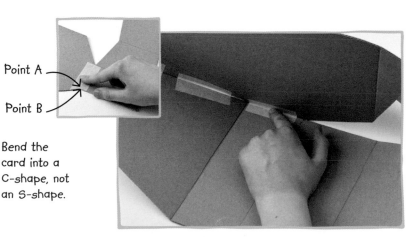

Point A

Point B

Bend the card into a C-shape, not an S-shape.

5 Now carefully crease the main piece along all its fold lines. Make sure your bends are all in the same direction.

6 Line up the point A of one of the two upper jaw pieces with point B on the main piece, and tape them together.

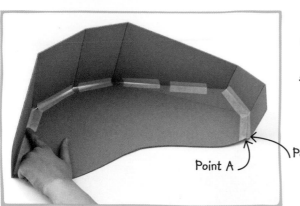

Point A   Point B

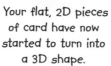

Your flat, 2D pieces of card have now started to turn into a 3D shape.

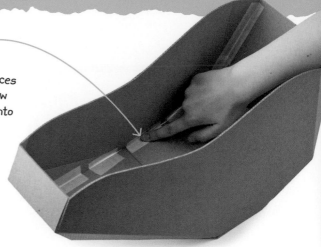

7 Carry on round, taping the two pieces together. Continue until all the straight edges of the upper jaw piece have been taped to the main piece.

8 Repeat steps 6–7 to attach the other upper jaw piece to the other side of the main piece; start by lining up point A and B as before.

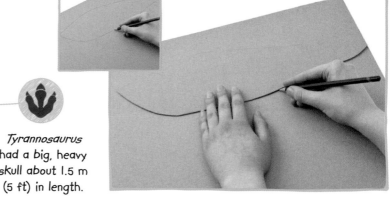

Tyrannosaurus had a big, heavy skull about 1.5 m (5 ft) in length.

9 Turn the head over and run a strip of masking tape along all the joins to make sure everything is securely taped together.

10 Draw a lower jaw piece onto craft card and cut it out. Then use it as a template for the second lower jaw piece, and cut that out too.

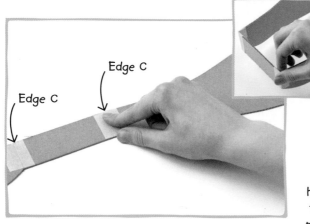

Edge C

Edge C

Tyrannosaurus had over 50 sharp teeth designed to puncture, tear, and slice flesh.

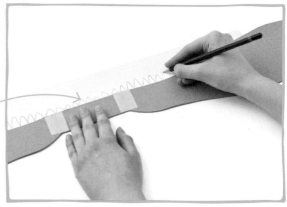

11 Draw and cut out the chin piece. Tape its short sides to the edges marked edge C on the template, to make a combined lower jaw section.

12 Place the lower jaw section on a long strip of white card, and draw a row of jagged teeth along the entire length of the top edge.

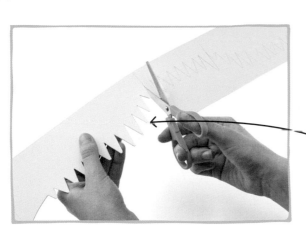

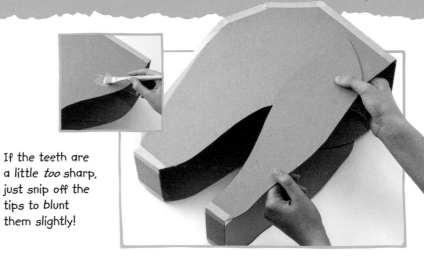

If the teeth are a little *too* sharp, just snip off the tips to blunt them slightly!

13 Carefully cut out this strip of teeth and the strip you drew for the upper side of the mouth in step 2.

14 Apply glue to the outside of the upper jaw pieces, as indicated on the template. Stick the lower jaw pieces firmly in place. Leave to set.

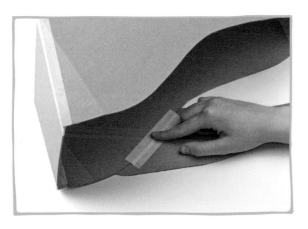

Tyrannosaurus jaws had huge muscles to deliver a powerful crushing bite.

15 Add a strip of masking tape to the join on the inside of the head too, to make sure the lower jaw is *securely* attached to the upper jaw.

16 Next, paint your *Tyrannosaurus* head all over with a base coat of green paint. You may need two coats. Leave to dry.

17 Draw a couple of rough oval shapes – one larger than the other – on a washing-up sponge and cut them out.

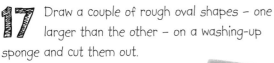

These ovals will form stamps to make patterns on the skin.

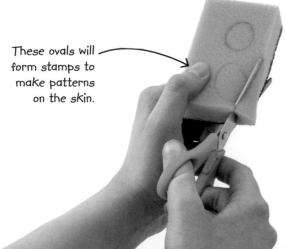

18 To paint the skin patterns, repeatedly dip the larger stamp in dark-green paint and dab it onto the mask.

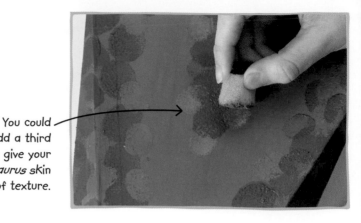

You could even add a third colour, to give your *Tyrannosaurus* skin lots of texture.

19 Once those marks are dry, repeat step 18 but using a mid-green paint and the smaller sponge stamp. Leave to dry.

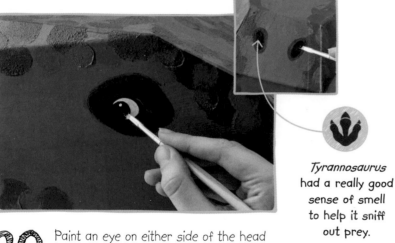

Tyrannosaurus had a really good sense of smell to help it sniff out prey.

20 Paint an eye on either side of the head (make sure they're level!), and paint the nostrils on the front end of the upper jaw.

21 Now paint the inside of the mask black. Start at the inside of the lower jaw and continue up into the whole head. Leave to dry.

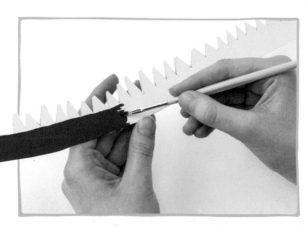

22 Paint both strips of teeth black below the jagged bits, so that they blend in with the black inside of the mask. Leave to dry.

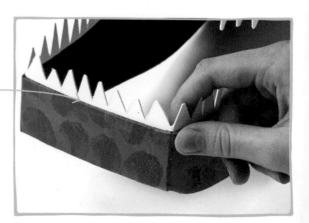

A *Tyrannosaurus* bite was at least four times the strength of an alligator's.

23 Apply glue to the non-black side of the lower-jaw strip, below the "teeth". Stick it along the inside of the lower jaw, and hold until set.

24 Repeat this process to stick the other strip of teeth to the upper jaw, so your *Tyrannosaurus* has two sets of fearsome teeth and is ready to hunt for prey!

This might *be* the last time you put your hand inside the mouth of a *Tyrannosaurus*!

Forward-facing eyes gave *Tyrannosaurus* 3D vision.

PREHISTORIC WORLD
ULTIMATE KILLING MACHINES

Tyrannosaurus teeth were bigger and stronger than those of any meat-eating dinosaur found so far. The biggest were 20 cm (8 in) long, and more like tusks than teeth. They had sharp points capable of piercing thick skin and muscle, but were deep-set in the jaw and tough enough to bite through bone. Scientists think that *Tyrannosaurus* attacked by taking a crippling bite of its prey, which would then be seriously injured or die of shock, leaving *Tyrannosaurus* to rip it apart and devour it.

Serrations on the side of *Tyrannosaurus* teeth helped spread the force of its bite, giving it the power to crush bone.

Thanks to its 3D vision, *Tyrannosaurus* was good at judging distances for an attack.

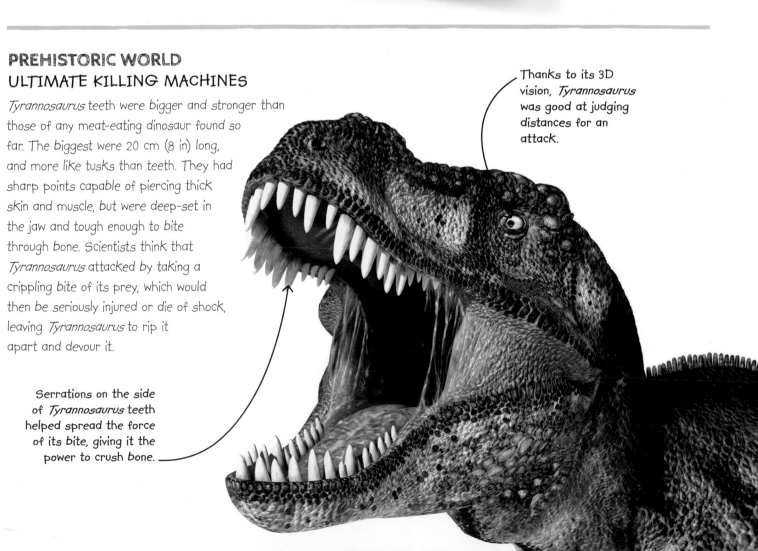

A SCARY TALE
TYRANNOSAURUS TAIL

Tyrannosaurus needed a strong, muscular tail to counterbalance its heavy head, so if you've made the mask, you'll need this impressive tail too. Decorate it to match the head and complete your transformation!

You wear the tail like a rucksack, with elastic straps over your shoulders.

If you've made the mask, just re-use the sponge stamps to paint the skin.

Tyrannosaurus held its tail roughly horizontal so it could run on its powerful hind legs.

Use clever paper engineering to make this tail stand out by itself.

MAKE YOUR OWN
DINO TAIL

For a perfect fit, measure across your shoulders, and from shoulder to waist. Use those measurements for the back pieces, and double them for the width and length of the tail piece.

Time 90 minutes, plus drying time

Difficulty Medium

WHAT YOU NEED

Pencil

Paintbrush

Scissors

Craft card

PVA glue

2 x elastic pieces

Masking tape

Stapler

Acrylic paints

Washing-up sponge

TEMPLATES

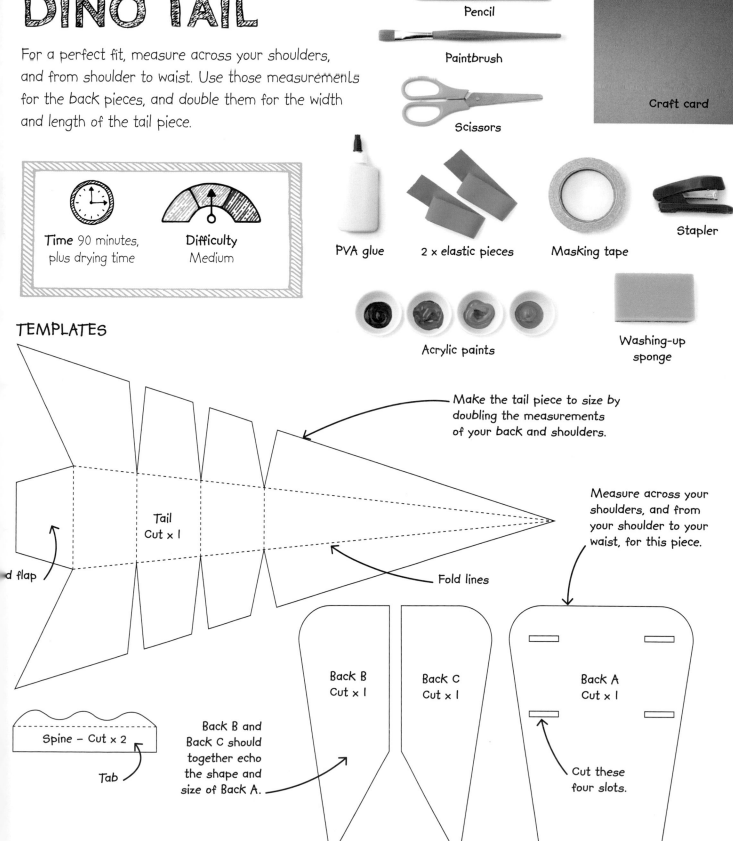

Tail
Cut x 1

Make the tail piece to size by doubling the measurements of your back and shoulders.

Measure across your shoulders, and from your shoulder to your waist, for this piece.

d flap

Fold lines

Spine – Cut x 2

Tab

Back B
Cut x 1

Back C
Cut x 1

Back A
Cut x 1

Back B and Back C should together echo the shape and size of Back A.

Cut these four slots.

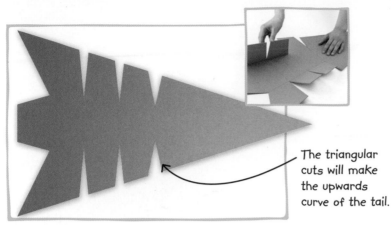

The triangular cuts will make the upwards curve of the tail.

1 Copy the template tail shape, cut it out, and bend the sides along the fold lines. Hold a ruler on the fold lines for extra-sharp creases.

2 Bring two sides of a tail section together and secure the join with masking tape. Continue along the tail, taping each section.

You're making a series of three-sided shapes called triangular polyhedrons.

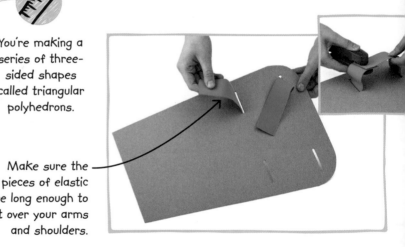

Make sure the pieces of elastic are long enough to fit over your arms and shoulders.

3 Bring two triangular polyhedrons together and tape them securely to each other. Repeat all along the tail, then tape up the end flap too.

4 Draw and cut out the three back pieces. Loop elastic through two slots on Back A, as shown, and staple together. Repeat for the second loop.

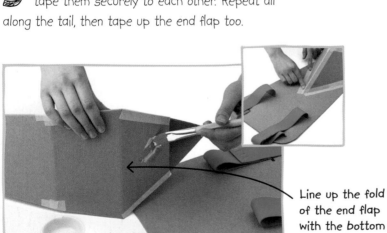

Line up the fold of the end flap with the bottom edge of Back A.

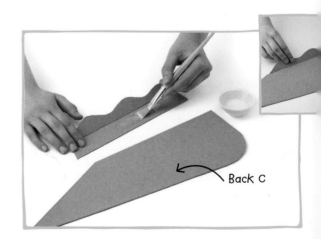

Back C

5 Glue the tail end flap to Back A and tape the joins to secure the tail piece in place. Then pull the two elastic loops through the slots so that the stapled joins sit flush against Back A.

6 Draw the two spine pieces and cut them out. Bend their tabs in opposite directions, and apply glue to each tab. Stick Back C onto one tab, as shown, and Back B onto the other.

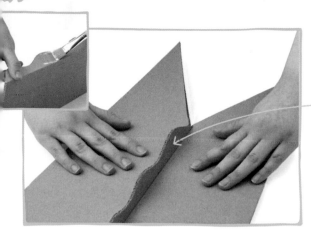

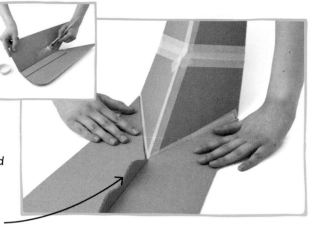

A strong spine helped *Tyrannosaurus* hold its tail horizontal.

7 Glue the two spine pieces together with the pointed ends of Back B and Back C facing the same way, so that they echo the shape of Back A.

Line up the tail and spine so that Back B and Back C sit neatly over Back A.

8 Glue the underside of Back B and Back C (the side without the spine showing). Stick it onto Back A, positioning it so that it fits around the tail piece, and press firmly until set.

9 Paint the tail and back section all over with the same base colour you used for the mask on page 93. Apply two coats if needed, then leave to dry.

10 Follow step 17 on page 93 to make sponge stamps, or use the ones you made for the mask. Use the biggest stamp to paint dark-green shapes, then apply a mid-green and any other colours you want with the smaller stamp. Leave to dry, then strap it on!

Fossils tell us that *Tyrannosaurus* skin was pebbled or bumpy.

Cluster the dots of skin markings along the spine and the top of the tail.

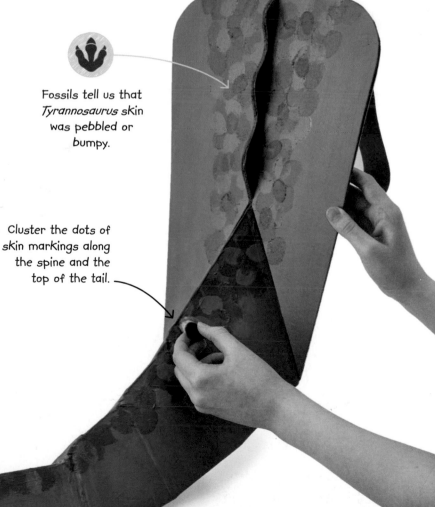

FOSSILS AND BONES

How do we know what we know about dinosaurs? Because of the fossils and other clues they left behind. Fossils are the remains of ancient life turned to stone, and they can reveal all sorts of important information about life on Earth millions of years ago. Create your own "fossils" as plaster, cookies, stencils, and jelly, make t-shirts and puzzle games, and enjoy exploring the exciting world of fossils.

FOSSIL COOKIES

Bake these edible "fossils" for a Triassic tea party. Fossils of dinosaur footprints, leaves, animals, and insects left important clues to what our planet was like millions of years ago. You could make these stamps for fossil footprint and ammonite cookies, then experiment with other fossil stamps too.

Trace fossils were those made by animal activity, such as tracks, nests, or dung.

Use icing to colour the footprints if you like.

Body fossils are those made by the bones or shell of an actual animal, such as this ammonite.

Dip your stamp in cocoa powder to add "mud" to your "fossil".

MAKE YOUR OWN
FOSSIL COOKIES

First, make the stamps; you'll need a polymer modelling clay that can be baked hard. Then get baking; this recipe makes 12 cookies. Ask an adult for help with the hot oven, and always wash your hands *before* making food.

Time 60 minutes, plus 10-12 minutes cooking time

Difficulty Medium

Warning Ask an adult to help you use the oven

WHAT YOU NEED

White paper

Baking trays

7 cm (2¾ in) cookie cutter

Marker pen

Modelling tool

Polymer modelling clay

Scissors

Baking parchment

Egg

1 teaspoon of vanilla extract

Large mixing bowl

100 g (3½ oz) caster sugar

Teaspoon measure

Scales

2 tbsp cocoa powder

Cup of water

Wooden spoon

Fork

100 g (3½ oz) butter

Rolling pin

4 tbsp icing sugar

Green food colouring

275 g (10 oz) plain flour (and extra for rolling out)

Tablespoon

Cooling rack

MAKE THE STAMPS

1 First, make the footprint. On a piece of paper, draw around your cookie cutter as a size guide. Sketch a footprint inside the circle.

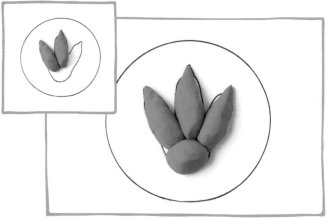

2 Roll small pieces of modelling clay to make the toes, and pinch the ends into claws. Position them on your sketch. Make a clay heel for the foot.

Make sure all the pieces are stuck together well.

3 Use a modelling tool (or the back of a teaspoon) to blend the pieces together.

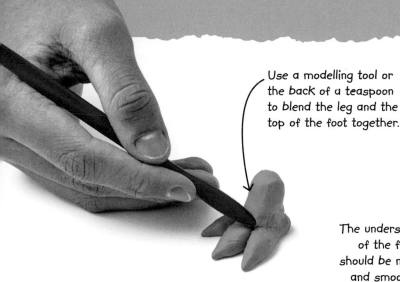

Use a modelling tool or the back of a teaspoon to blend the leg and the top of the foot together.

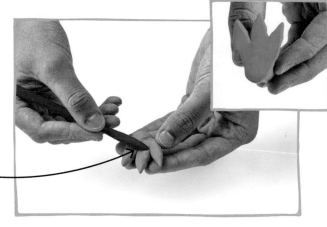

The underside of the foot should be nice and smooth.

4 Roll a small piece of clay and stick it to the top of the foot to make the leg.

5 Carefully turn over the foot to make sure the clay is fully worked together and the underside is as smooth as possible too.

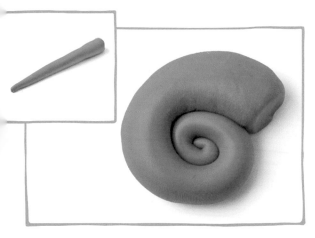

6 To make the ammonite fossil, roll a ball of clay into a long sausage shape with one end thinner than the other. Coil it into a spiral, and make sure it fits inside the cookie cutter.

7 Using the modelling tool or a fork, work your way around the spiral, marking straight lines across the clay.

An ammonite's shell enlarged as it grew, forming a beautiful hollow spiral.

9 Ask an adult to take the baked stamps out of the oven. Leave them to cool. The baking should have made them really hard.

8 Put the foot and ammonite onto a parchment-lined baking tray. Bake in the oven following the manufacturer's instructions.

MAKE THE COOKIES

Let the butter soften before you start, so it's easier to mix with the sugar.

1 Mix the butter and sugar together in a large bowl. Beat the egg in a small bowl with a fork, then add it to the butter and sugar, a little at a time.

2 Once they are all mixed together, add the vanilla extract. Ask an adult to preheat the oven to 180°C (350°F/Gas 4).

3 Add the flour, a few tablespoons at a time, and stir together until the mixture becomes a firm ball (you might find it easier to do the last bit with your hands).

Sprinkling a little flour on the worktop stops your dough sticking when you roll it out.

4 Roll out the dough with the rolling pin until it's about 0.5 cm (¼ in) thick. Cut out the cookies with the cutter. Squish the leftover dough back into a ball, re-roll, and cut out more cookies.

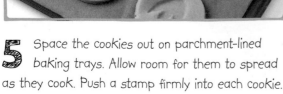

Remove the stamp carefully to leave a clear print in the dough.

5 Space the cookies out on parchment-lined baking trays. Allow room for them to spread as they cook. Push a stamp firmly into each cookie.

6 If you want to make "muddy" fossils, dip your stamp into cocoa powder. Be gentle, so that cocoa powder doesn't go everywhere!

Move your cookies carefully so they don't break.

7 Once you have stamped all the cookies, bake them in the oven for 10–12 mins, until golden-brown. Ask an adult to take them out of the oven.

8 Leave the cookies for 10 mins before transferring them onto a rack to cool completely.

Add a tiny drop of green food colouring if you want "swampy" footprints.

Make sure the icing goes right to the end of the toes.

9 Mix the icing sugar with a few drops of water at a time, until it forms a thick-ish pouring consistency. If you want a colour other than white, add a tiny drop of food colouring.

10 Once the cookies are cold, carefully pour icing into the footprints you want to colour. Allow the icing to set, then share the cookies with your friends and enjoy!

PREHISTORIC WORLD
HOW FOSSILS FORM

Fossils need certain conditions in order to form. First, the leaf, insect, or animal (such as this ammonite), need to lie undisturbed in mud or sand (sediment). As it decays, layers of mud and sand build up over it. Water seeps through the layers, replacing the decayed material with minerals that turn the fossil into rock. Millions of years pass. Eventually, glaciers or weather may erode the surrounding sedimentary rock to reveal the fossil.

PLASTER FOSSILS

A trace left in the mud – a discarded shell, a fallen leaf, a dead starfish or insect – can over millions of years turn into a solid rock fossil waiting to be discovered. Luckily, these fake fossils can be made in just a weekend.

Paint your "fossils" to make them look like they've been buried for millions of years.

Collect leaves and shells to make your "fossils".

MAKE YOUR OWN
FOSSIL

To create your fossil you'll make a cardboard mould and use plaster of Paris, a powder that becomes a thick liquid when mixed with water, then sets hard like rock. For safety, ask an adult for help when mixing it.

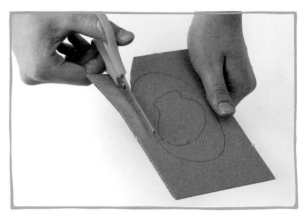

1 To make the mould *base*, draw around your "fossil" object on the stiff card. Sketch a larger oval shape around the outline and cut it out.

2 Cut a strip of thin card about 5 cm (2 in) wide and long enough to wrap around the edge of the *base*. Tape the strip all around the *base*.

3 Once you have attached card all around the *base*, overlap the ends by about 1 cm (²⁄₅ in), then trim off any remaining card. Seal the join with a strip of tape.

Time	30 minutes, plus drying time
Difficulty	Easy
Warning	Ask an adult for help with plaster of Paris

WHAT YOU NEED

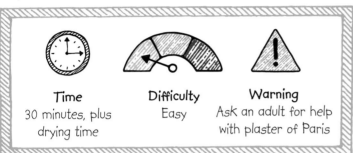

Pencil

Scissors

Masking tape

Plasticine

Thin card

Tablespoon

Stiff card

Acrylic paint

Shell or other "fossil" object

Modelling tool or teaspoon

(Empty yoghurt pot or other disposable container)

Plaster of Paris

Cup of water

Kitchen towel

Paintbrush

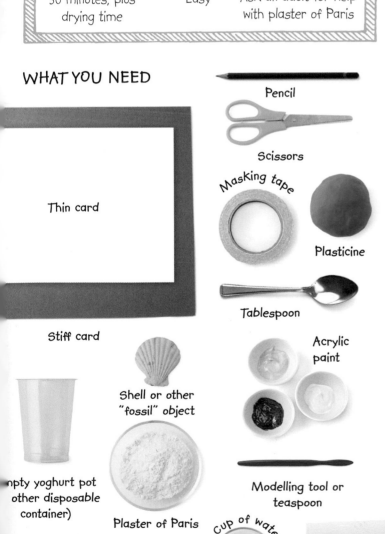

Make the plasticine layer thicker than your "fossil" object.

Real fossils were created by imprints or objects left in mud millions of years ago.

4 Soften some plasticine in your hands. Press a layer of it inside the mould, deep enough for the object to be pushed into, then smooth it out.

5 Push your "fossil" object firmly into the plasticine to make a clear, clean imprint, then carefully remove it without damaging the imprint.

Let any left-over mixture harden, then throw it away in the container – do not pour it down the drain.

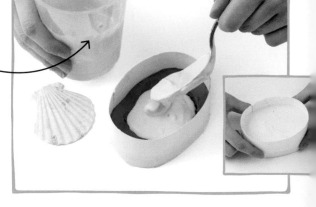

6 Mix up one cup of water and one cup of plaster of Paris in the yoghurt pot (or any container you don't mind throwing away afterwards).

7 Carefully spoon enough mix into the mould to make a layer of plaster about 1 cm (²⁄₅ in) deep. Tap the mould on a table to get rid of air bubbles.

9 Gently remove the plasticine layer to reveal the "cast fossil".

8 Leave to dry for two hours, until the plaster is almost set, then carefully peel away the cardboard strip and the base of the mould.

The plaster has filled the imprint you made in the plasticine.

10 While the plaster is still a little bit damp, smooth the edges with a modelling tool or back of a teaspoon. Leave for 24 hours to harden fully.

11 Mix beige and white paint to make a pale rock colour. Paint the fossil with a base coat, then leave to dry.

Cast fossils take their shape from spaces in mud filled by minerals that gradually turn into rock.

Wipe off most of the paint so it is only in the grooves and details.

12 Mix a little water and dark brown paint into a thin solution. Paint the fossil, then wipe much of it off again with kitchen towel. Leave to dry.

13 To finish, neaten up the final fossil by carefully painting around the edge with your original base colour.

PREHISTORIC WORLD
TYPES OF FOSSIL

Although they all take millions of years to form, there are different types of fossil. Trace fossils are made by animal activity such as droppings or footprints in mud. Body fossils form in impressions left in rock when a leaf or creature rots completely; if it fills with rock minerals, it's called a cast fossil. Sometimes, something is preserved whole as a true form fossil, either in ice or amber (hardened tree sap).

Hard tissue such as bones can rot slowly to be replaced by rock-forming minerals.

Coprolites (fossilized dung) can contain clues about what dinosaurs ate.

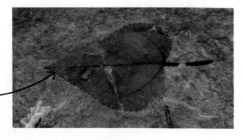

The impression of this dried leaf in mud millions of years ago even retained its colour.

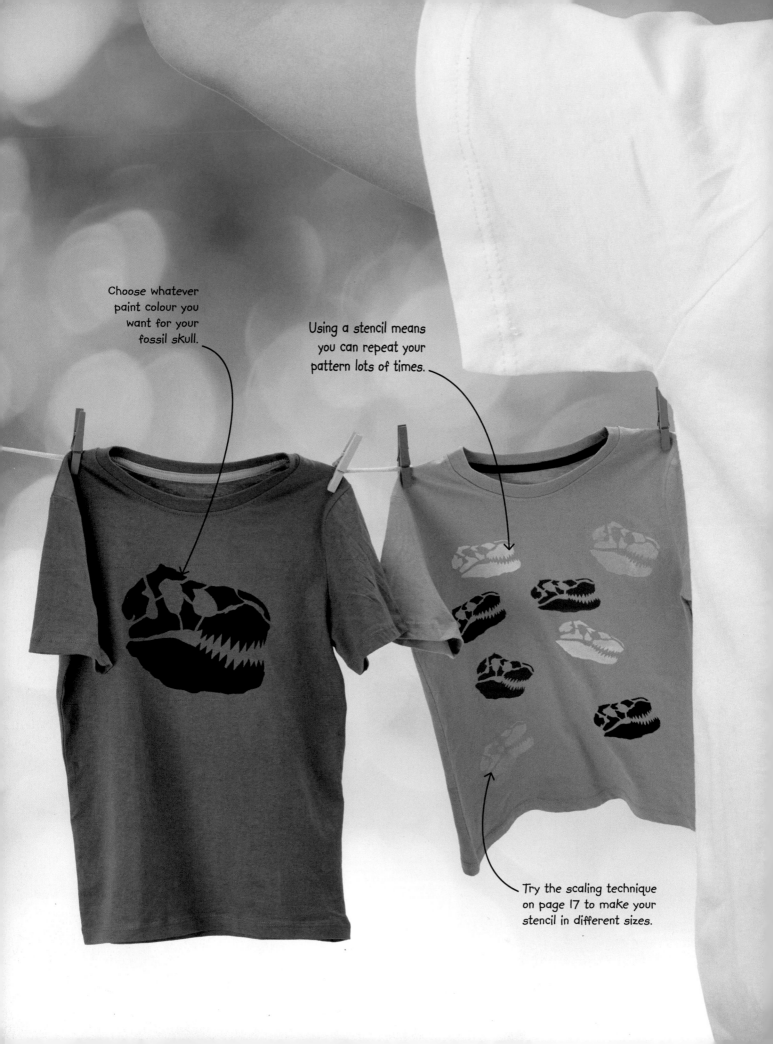

Choose whatever
paint colour you
want for your
fossil skull.

Using a stencil means
you can repeat your
pattern lots of times.

Try the scaling technique
on page 17 to make your
stencil in different sizes.

You can use two paint colours to give your fossil skull added "depth".

Tyrannosaurus fossils show that much of its skull was taken up with huge, terrifying jaws.

STENCIL POWER
TYRANNOSAURUS FOSSIL T-SHIRT

Body fossils of dinosaurs have helped fill in some of the gaps in our knowledge of how a dinosaur lived, moved, bred, and found food. Fill in the different kind of gaps between this stencil to make your own fossil-patterned t-shirt.

MAKE YOUR OWN
FOSSIL SKULL T-SHIRT

Stencils work by filling in the spaces between shapes; just remember to have connecting strips to hold the "holes" in place. Any card will do, as long as its thick enough to stop paint seeping through it.

WHAT YOU NEED

Stencil card

Stiff card

T-shirt

Plasticine

Pencil

Masking tape

Scissors

Clothes pegs

Iron

Fabric paints

Stencil brush

Time
90 minutes, plus drying time

Difficulty
Medium

Warning
Ask an adult for help with the iron

TEMPLATE

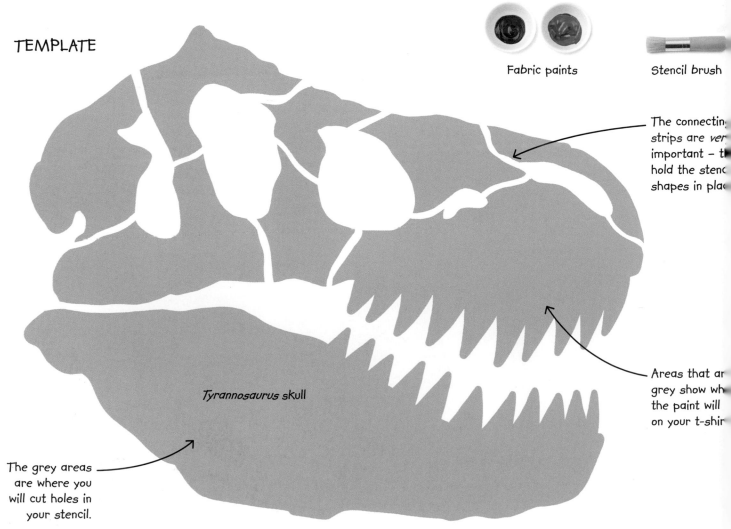

Tyrannosaurus skull

The connecting strips are *very* important – they hold the stencil shapes in place

Areas that are grey show where the paint will go on your t-shirt

The grey areas are where you will cut holes in your stencil.

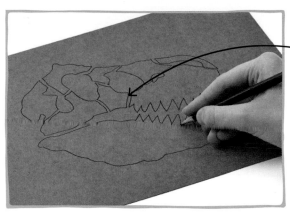

These are the connecting strips that hold the stencil together.

1 Draw (or trace) the skull template onto stencil card. Make sure you include all the little connecting strips.

2 With protective plasticine behind the card, carefully make a hole with a pencil in each of the areas coloured grey on the template.

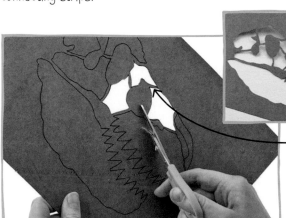

Take care around the connecting strips, as they create the holes for your paint.

3 Insert your scissors carefully into each of the pencil holes and cut out all the areas coloured grey on the template.

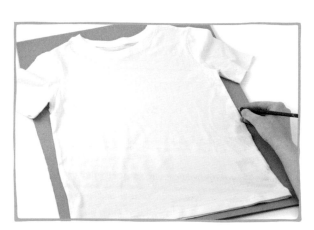

4 Mark the width of your t-shirt on a piece of stiff card and cut the card so that it is as wide as your t-shirt.

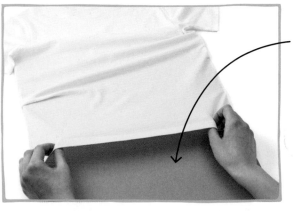

The card is to stop paint seeping through to the back of your t-shirt.

5 Pull the t-shirt down over the card, sliding the card between the front and back to act as a barrier against the paint.

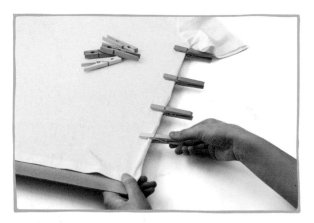

6 Smooth the t-shirt flat, and then place clothes pegs down the sides to hold it securely in position against the card.

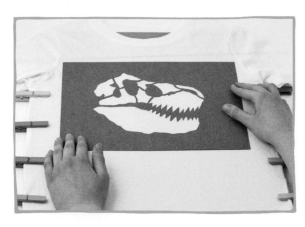

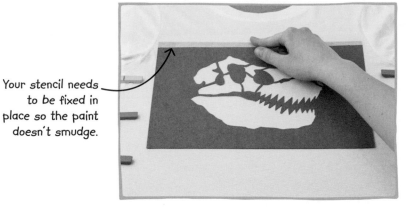

7 Position your stencil where you would like it on your t-shirt (we've done ours on the front, but you could put it on the back if you wish).

Your stencil needs to be fixed in place so the paint doesn't smudge.

8 Secure the stencil across the top with a strip of masking tape and press along it to make sure it's firmly stuck down.

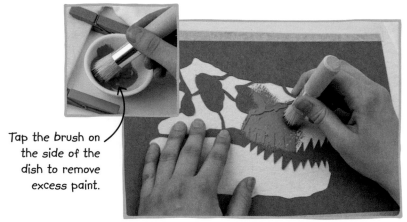

Tap the brush on the side of the dish to remove excess paint.

9 Add another strip of masking tape along the bottom of the stencil to fix it securely in position on the t-shirt.

10 Dip your brush into the fabric paint and dab it carefully onto the t-shirt. Hold the stencil flat with the other hand.

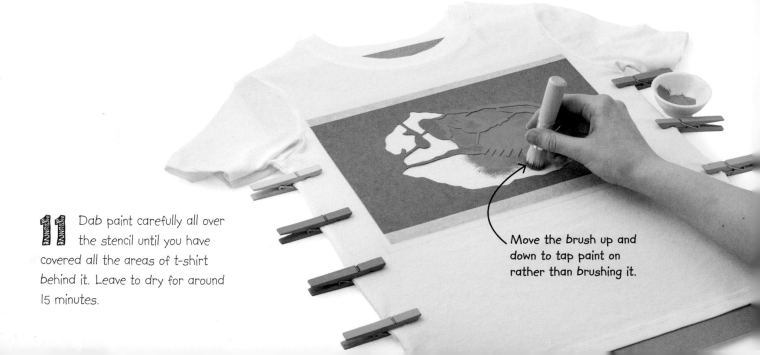

11 Dab paint carefully all over the stencil until you have covered all the areas of t-shirt behind it. Leave to dry for around 15 minutes.

Move the brush up and down to tap paint on rather than brushing it.

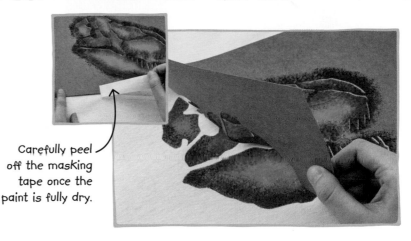

Carefully peel off the masking tape once the paint is fully dry.

12 Mix a darker paint colour and dab it around the edges of the stencil holes to give the *skull* some texture. Leave to dry.

13 Gently remove the masking tape and carefully lift off the stencil to reveal your fossil skull.

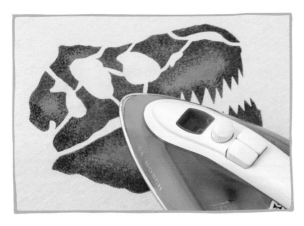

Tyrannosaurus actually had large holes in its *skull*, which helped make it lighter.

14 Ask an adult to iron the t-shirt for 5 minutes, to "fix" the fabric paint so that it won't run in the wash.

15 Remove the stiff card and put your t-shirt on. You could reuse the stencil to make a whole herd of fossil t-shirts for your friends too!

PREHISTORIC WORLD
WHAT A SKULL CAN TELL US

A *Tyrannosaurus* skull could weigh a hefty 500 kg (1,100 lb), despite large holes, called "fenestrae", that helped lighten the weight of it and made room for powerful jaw muscles. Large dinosaurs like *Tyrannosaurus* were at risk of overheating, and the fenestrae in the front of the *skull* housed huge air sinuses that probably played a role in temperature control.

Tyrannosaurus skull was wider at the back to make room for the massive jaw muscles that powered its bite.

GAME OF BONES

FOSSIL SKELETON PUZZLE

What does it feel like to discover a dinosaur fossil? Make this salt-dough skeleton, bury it in a tray of sand, then go fossil-hunting for bones and try to solve the puzzle of what goes where.

Salt dough is modelling clay that you can make at home from just flour, water, and salt.

Work out how to assemble the individual "bones" of your puzzle into a complete skeleton.

Hide the "bones"
jumbled-up in a
tray of sand, ready
for a fossil-hunt.

MAKE YOUR OWN
SALT-DOUGH DINO PUZZLE

Photograph or photocopy the template below and print it out at whatever size you want your dino bones to be. This project uses dough, but it's far too salty to eat!

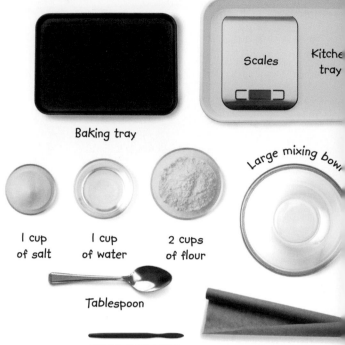

WHAT YOU NEED

Baking tray

Scales

Kitche tray

Large mixing bowl

1 cup of salt

1 cup of water

2 cups of flour

Tablespoon

Modelling tools

Parchment paper

Oven gloves

Sand

Time
45 minutes, plus cooking time

Difficulty
Easy

Warning
Ask an adult to help you use the oven

TEMPLATE

Make a salt-dough piece for each of the black areas on the template.

1 Mix the salt and flour together in a large bowl, then make a hollow in the centre and pour in the cup of water. Mix it all together with the spoon.

The ball should feel like soft modelling clay when you have finished.

2 Use your hands to knead the dough for about 3–4 minutes until it all comes together in a ball. Add a bit more flour if the mix seems too sticky.

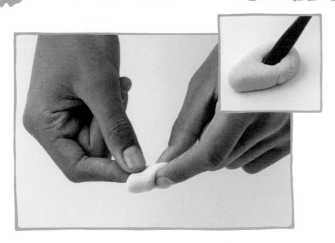

3 Break off a small piece of dough and start moulding the bones with your fingers or modelling tools – whatever works best for you!

4 Using your template as a guide, make and assemble all the different pieces of the skeleton puzzle. Lay the pieces in position as you do them, to be sure you've made them all.

The bones are ready when, they're hard; – ask an adult to check for you.

5 Lay the bones on a baking tray lined with parchment paper. Bake them in the oven at 150°C (300°F/Gas 2) for about 30–60 mins, depending how thick the pieces are.

6 Once the pieces have cooled down completely, bury them in a kitchen tray filled with sand. Then begin the hunt for the bones of your fossil skeleton puzzle.

PREHISTORIC WORLD
A REAL-LIFE FOSSIL PUZZLE

In around 1909, in a quarry in Utah, USA, palaeontologists (scientists who study fossils) found a massive puzzle of fossil bones. About 150 million years ago, the site had been a river system, and the jumble of bones was probably the result of animals dying there during droughts. Now called the Dinosaur National Monument, it has a wall of more than 1,500 fossil bones from different dinosaurs.

FOSSIL TREATS
JELLY AMBER

A party treat made of hardened tree sap full of really, really old dead insects? That definitely doesn't sound like something you'd want to serve your friends, but they'll love this version instead, with jelly "amber" and currant "insects".

This jelly mixture uses agar agar, a powder that absorbs water molecules.

Your "insects" are held in the middle of the jelly.

MAKE YOUR OWN
JELLY AMBER

This jelly uses agar agar, which is actually made from red and purple seaweed (but don't worry, it doesn't taste of it!). It is vegetarian, and comes as powder or flakes.

Time	Difficulty	Warning
30 minutes, plus setting time	Easy	Ask an adult to help you use the hob

WHAT YOU NEED

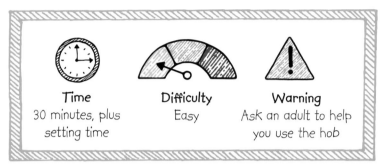

Silicone ice-cube tray

Vegetable oil

Orange food colouring

Orange food flavouring

1 tablespoon agar agar powder

Pastry brush

Tablespoon

Jug of 350 ml (12 fl oz) cold water

Currants

Saucepan

Cocktail sticks

Trivet

525 g (18½ oz) white caster sugar

Small bowls

1 Lightly brush the insides of the ice-cube moulds with vegetable oil. This will make your jelly amber easier to get out once it has set.

2 Gently squish some currants to make insect shapes. Pull some into "spiders" or "flies", for example, and squash others into flat "beetles".

3 Add orange food colouring to the cold water, one drop at a time, until the water is amber-coloured. Then add the flavouring, a drop at a time too (you can taste it to check).

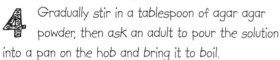

Stir until the powder has all dissolved into the water.

4 Gradually stir in a tablespoon of agar agar powder, then ask an adult to pour the solution into a pan on the hob and bring it to boil.

5 Ask the adult to remove the pan from the heat and stand it on a trivet. Gradually stir in the caster sugar, being careful of the hot liquid.

Real amber is made from tree sap that flows from a wound in the tree bark.

6 Keep stirring until all the sugar has dissolved and you have a completely clear liquid with no crystals in it.

7 Ask the adult to pour the liquid back into the jug, as it is a lot easier to fill the ice-cube tray from the jug than from the saucepan.

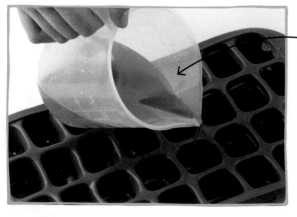

Pour carefully and steadily to smoothly fill the moulds.

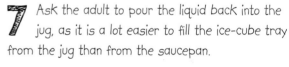

8 Carefully pour the mixture into each mould in the ice-cube tray. Hold the jug low to minimize the chances of creating air bubbles.

9 Wiggle a cocktail stick around in each mould if you need to dislodge any air bubbles. Leave for 30 minutes in a cool place to partially set.

If the jellies "bounce" slightly when pressed, they are ready.

10 After about 30 minutes, gently test with a clean finger to check that the jellies are partially set – no longer liquid but not solid yet.

11 Use a cocktail stick to gently push a currant "insect" down into the middle of each mould. Don't push too far – just halfway down.

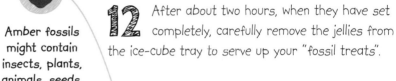

Amber fossils might contain insects, plants, animals, seeds, and even pollen.

12 After about two hours, when they have set completely, carefully remove the jellies from the ice-cube tray to serve up your "fossil treats".

PREHISTORIC WORLD
THE SAP TRAP

Trees can produce a sticky liquid sap that hardens to become amber. Insects trapped in prehistoric tree sap before it hardened have been preserved so perfectly in it that even the veins in their wings are visible, like in the picture below. They look almost still alive, but may be more than 100 million years old! And it's not just insects that have been fossilized in amber; scientists have found birds, a hatchling, and even portions of dinosaur tail too.

Carefully lift each jelly out by pushing the mould from underneath.

DINOSAUR PLANET

Wouldn't it be amazing to be a time-traveller and go back millions of years to see the Earth as it was when the dinosaurs roamed, grazed, and hunted? In this chapter, you can recreate that world for yourself. Grow a Jurassic jungle in a jar; build your own layers of "sediment", just like the Earth does; create an underwater hunting ground in a box; and make your own erupting volcano. It's thought that the reign of the dinosaurs ended when a giant meteorite struck Earth, so finish the chapter with your own meteorite experiment.

SEDIMENTARY ROCK CAKE

Sedimentary rock is the key to so much of what we know about dinosaurs and prehistoric life, as it is where most fossils have been found. Just as sediment builds up layer by layer, you too will build up your cake in layers. Then cut a slice and enjoy!

If this were real sedimentary rock, you might find a fossilized dinosaur in one of the layers.

Your edible "sedimentary layers" develop just like rocks, rubble, and mud do – but much faster.

MAKE YOUR OWN
SEDIMENTARY ROCK CAKE

Layer up cereals instead of sand and gravel, and marsh-mallows instead of mud, to build six tiers of "sediment" for this cake. It is very sweet, so serve it in small slices.

Time	Difficulty	Warning
60 minutes, plus setting time	Easy	Ask an adult to help you use the hob

WHAT YOU NEED

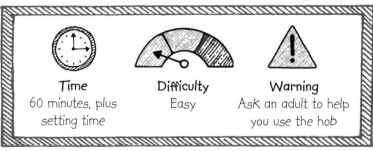

Pastry brush   Vegetable oil   Square dish

Saucepan   Scales   ↑Trivet

Wooden spoon

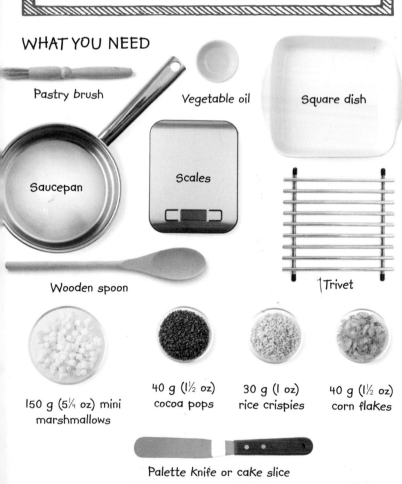

150 g (5¼ oz) mini marshmallows

40 g (1½ oz) cocoa pops

30 g (1 oz) rice crispies

40 g (1½ oz) corn flakes

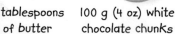
Palette knife or cake slice

tablespoons of butter

100 g (4 oz) white chocolate chunks

100 g (4 oz) dark chocolate chunks

100 g (4 oz) milk chocolate chunks

1 Brush the inside of the dish lightly with vegetable oil. This will stop the cake sticking to the dish, so you can get it out easily.

2 Melt a tablespoon of butter and 50 g (1¾ oz) of mini marshmallows together in a saucepan over a low heat. Take it off the heat as soon as they have melted, and stir to blend them together.

3 Add 40 g (1½ oz) of cocoa pops to the pan. They will become the first "sedimentary layer" of your cake.

Stir gently so your "rocks" don't turn to rubble.

4 Stir thoroughly to coat the cocoa pops in the melted mixture.

5 Spoon the mixture into the dish and press it down gently to form a flat layer.

Butter and marshmallows are solids that turn into liquids when melted, but then set solid again when cooled.

Layers of sediment buried leaves and creatures that were then fossilized within them.

6 Sprinkle 100 g (4 oz) of white chocolate chunks on top and press firmly into the mixture. You have now made two layers of "sediment".

7 Repeat step 2, melting the same amounts of butter and marshmallows together. Then stir 40 g (1½ oz) of corn flakes into the mixture.

Make sure the layer is flat and level into each corner.

8 Spoon the mixture on top of the white chocolate layer. Press firmly to crush the corn flakes and flatten out the mixture.

9 Sprinkle 100 g (4 oz) of dark chocolate chunks over the corn flake mixture and push them in firmly to make your fourth "sedimentary layer".

Stir gently again this time, to avoid crushing your "rocks".

10 Repeat step 2, melting the same amounts of butter and marshmallows on the hob. This time, stir in 30 g (1 oz) of rice crispies.

11 Again, make sure the ingredients are completely mixed together, then spread the mixture on top of the dark chocolate layer.

13 Leave to set in a cool place for a couple of hours, then your sedimentary rock cake is ready to slice up and serve.

12 Finally, sprinkle 100 g (4 oz) of milk chocolate chunks over the rice crispie mixture and push them down to make your sixth layer.

PREHISTORIC WORLD
THE LAW OF SUPERPOSITION

Sedimentary rock is where scientists discover the fossils that tell them so much about the prehistoric world. Traces of prehistoric life can be fossilized between layers of sand, mud, and gravel that have built up over millions of years. Geologists (scientists who study the Earth's structure and surface) know that these layers are created according to something called the Law of Superposition. That law states that each layer of sediment (or "stratum") is younger than the layers below it, and older than the layers above it – just like the layers in your cake, with the bottom layers being the "oldest"!

AN OCEAN IN A BOX
MARINE DIORAMA

While the first dinosaurs were walking on land, the Triassic seas teemed with marine life, including reptiles such as *Nothosaurus*, as well as many other creatures, from sharks and bony fish to squid and ammonites. How many can you fit into a shoe-box diorama?

Almost-invisible threads hold the sea creatures in place.

Position creatures to fit their behaviour; for example, this *Placodus* hunted for shellfish on the seabed.

Nothosaurus had to pop its head above water to breathe, so you could burst its head above the "waterline" of your diorama.

Making some ammonites larger than others creates the illusion that some are closer.

Three "layers" of seabed trick your eyes and create a sense of distance.

MAKE YOUR OWN
MARINE DIORAMA

We've chosen *Nothosaurus* and creatures that lived alongside it, but you can research other marine creatures online if you wish. Think about scale, and make some creatures smaller to trick your brain into thinking that they are further away.

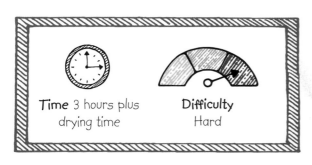

Time 3 hours plus drying time

Difficulty Hard

WHAT YOU NEED

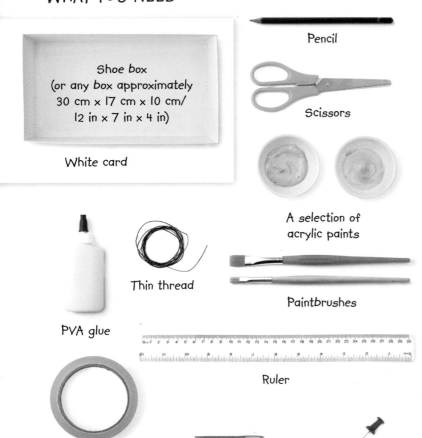

Shoe box
(or any box approximately
30 cm x 17 cm x 10 cm/
12 in x 7 in x 4 in)

White card

Pencil

Scissors

A selection of acrylic paints

Thin thread

Paintbrushes

PVA glue

Ruler

Adhesive tape   Darning needle   Pinboard pin

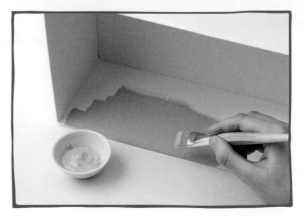

1 Paint the inside of a long side of the shoe box with sand-coloured paint. This will be your base.

2 Paint the rest of the box with blue paint, inside and out. You may find that you need to repeat steps 1–2 if the box needs two coats of paint. Leave to dry.

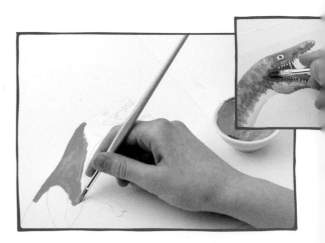

3 Draw your main marine creature (we've chosen a *Nothosaurus*). Paint a base coat, then add dappled skin markings and other details, such as eyes and teeth.

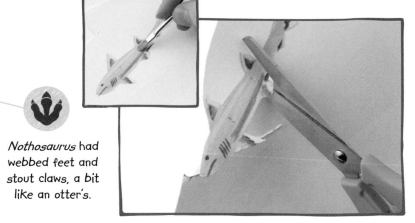

 4 When the paint is dry, carefully cut around the outline of the *Nothosaurus*.

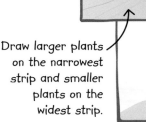

Nothosaurus had webbed feet and stout claws, a bit like an otter's.

5 Repeat steps 3-4 to make all the other creatures for your diorama.

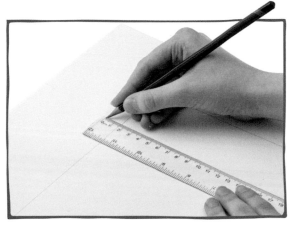

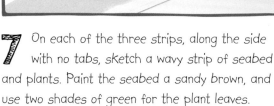

Draw larger plants on the narrowest strip and smaller plants on the widest strip.

6 Draw a rectangle the length of the box base, and 5 cm (2 in) wide. Draw tabs 1.5 cm (⅝ in) wide on three sides. Draw two more strips the same length, but make each one a little narrower.

7 On each of the three strips, along the side with no tabs, sketch a wavy strip of seabed and plants. Paint the seabed a sandy brown, and use two shades of green for the plant leaves.

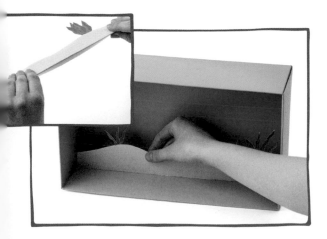

Making the plants smaller at the back creates an illusion of distance.

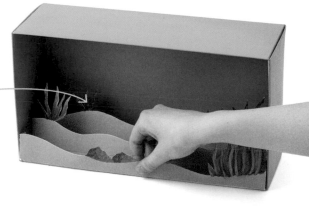

8 When the paint is dry, cut each strip out and bend the tabs away from the painted sides. Glue the three tabs of the widest strip to the sides and base of the box, near the back.

9 Next, glue the second strip into position about halfway inside the box, and finish by gluing the narrowest strip in line with the front edge of the box.

10 Hold the *Nothosaurus* in front of the box with its head "above water". Mark where the top of the box crosses its neck, and cut there.

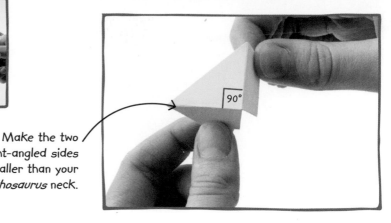

Make the two right-angled sides smaller than your *Nothosaurus* neck.

11 On white card, draw a small right-angled triangle. Add 1.5 cm (⅝ in) tabs on the right-angled sides. Cut it out and fold the tabs.

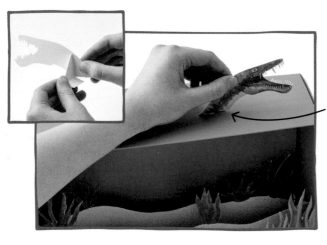

Glue the neck near one side, so there's room for the body inside the box.

12 Glue one tab to the back of the neck and the other halfway across the top of the box, to hold the head "above water".

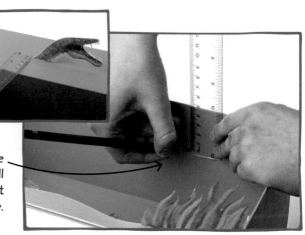

This marks the spot where you'll stick the rest of the body.

13 Measure the distance from the neck to the front of the box. Mark the same distance from the front on the underside.

Line the fold up with the cut edge of the neck.

14 Cut a strip of card about 4 cm (1½ in) long and slightly thinner than the neck. Fold it in half, glue one half, and stick it to the body.

15 Glue the other half of the strip and stick it at the mark you made in step 13, lining up the neck above and below the top side of the box.

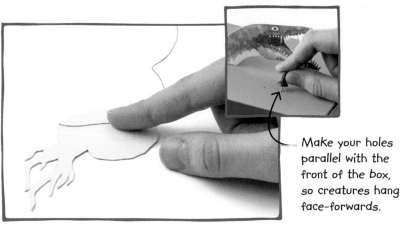

Make your holes parallel with the front of the box, so creatures hang face-forwards.

16 Tape one end of some thread to the back of your next creature. Thread the other end through a needle. Use the pin to make two holes, 1.5 cm (⅝ in) apart, in the top of the box.

17 Push the needle up through the left hole and down through the right one. Remove the needle and position the creature at the height you want it, with the thread hanging behind.

18 Tape the loose thread onto the back of the card so that the creature faces forward when it hangs loose. Cut the thread to length, with the end hidden behind the creature.

19 Repeat steps 16-18 to position all your remaining sea creatures. Paint white splashes on the top of the box to show the *Nothosaurus* bursting out of the water.

PREHISTORIC WORLD ON LAND AND SEA

Nothosaurus was an early marine reptile of the Triassic period. Like a seal, it hunted at sea but probably came ashore to rest and breed. It could drive itself through the water with its powerful tail, but those webbed feet could also clamber over rocky shores. Its flexible neck and needle-sharp teeth were ideal for swinging through the water to snap up nearby fish.

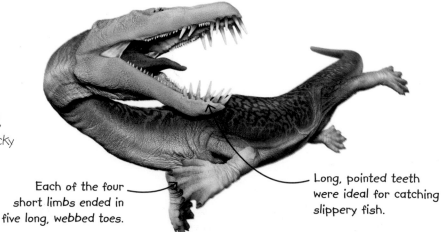

Each of the four short limbs ended in five long, webbed toes.

Long, pointed teeth were ideal for catching slippery fish.

JURASSIC JUNGLE JAR

There are plants growing today that would not have looked unfamiliar to the dinosaurs roaming Jurassic Earth. Learn about the plants we share with the Earth of 150 million years ago, and create a mini prehistoric world in which your dinosaur collection would feel at home.

Have any small dinosaurs that need a home? They'll love this terrarium!

Collect small stones that will make great "rocks" for your mini Jurassic world.

Think about scale – a small fern in a pot can look like a tree in your mini-world.

MAKE YOUR OWN
PREHISTORIC TERRARIUM

There are several small plants you can choose from that had Jurassic relatives, such as ferns, mosses, and horsetails. The amounts of grit and other materials below are approximate and will depend on the size of your jar and the plants you choose. Use a flat-bottomed jar if possible.

Time
30 minutes

Difficulty
Easy

These layers stop the roots rotting, so they can supply water and nutrients to the plants.

WHAT YOU NEED

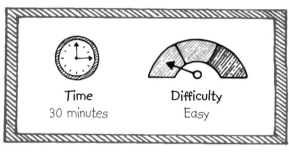

12 tablespoons of pebbles

13 tablespoons of sand

10 tablespoons of grit

16 tablespoons of compost

Large glass jar (about 30 cm/1 ft high)

Tablespoon

6 tablespoons of small light-coloured pebbles

Paintbrush

"Jurassic" plants

"Jurassic" toys

Small stones

1 Carefully spread a layer of pebbles about 2 cm (¾ in) deep over the base of your jar. Don't just drop them in as they might break it.

2 Next, spoon over a layer of sand about 2 cm (¾ in) deep. Tap the side of the jar gently to settle it, and smooth it out to make sure it's even.

3 Add a 2 cm (¾ in) layer of grit, spooning it in carefully to avoid disturbing the sand. Again, smooth it out so the surface is even.

4 Now add a layer of compost about 4–5 cm (1½–2 in) deep. There's no need to smooth it down as you will be planting into it.

Scoop out a hole for each plant with the tablespoon or your hands.

5 Carefully remove the plants from their pots and plant them into the soil. Think about how to arrange them so you can see them all.

Use a paintbrush to brush any soil off the glass.

6 Once you are happy with the positioning of the plants, add a final layer of light-coloured pebbles around the plants. Take care not to put stones on top of the plants.

7 To finish, add a few slightly larger stones, your favourite dinosaur, or the fossils you made on pages 108–111. Water your terrarium occasionally – only when the compost looks dry.

PREHISTORIC WORLD
JURASSIC SURVIVORS

During the Jurassic Period, the Earth very gradually transformed from a hot, arid planet to become more green and lush, and some of the plants that grew then are very similar to those growing today. Ginkgo and monkey-puzzle trees, for example, have hardly changed since they first grew in Jurassic China. Modern-day ferns, conifers, cycads, mosses, and horsetails are all survivors of plant families that grew alongside dinosaurs.

CRYSTAL GEODES

Hidden in air bubbles trapped in molten lava as it turned to rock, or in air pockets between layers of sedimentary rock, there may be a secret – beautiful crystals called "geodes". Astonishingly, geodes have even been found in the spaces within dinosaur bone fossils! Real geodes take thousands of years to form, but you can make fake ones in a few days.

The longer you leave them to grow, the more crystals you will have in your geode.

Make your geodes in different colours, just like nature does.

MAKE YOUR OWN
GEODE

The key ingredient you need to "grow" your geode is alum, a chemical compound that forms crystals in water. The food colouring you add to the water gives the crystals their colour. You can easily get alum at a pharmacy or online, but keep it away from your eyes and mouth, and wash your hands afterwards. Ask an adult for help with the boiling water.

Time 60 minutes, plus 12–24 hours soaking, and drying time

Difficulty Easy

Warning Keep alum away from eyes and mouth. Get help with hot water.

WHAT YOU NEED

Small bowls

Egg

Darning needle

150 g (5 oz) alum in a shallow bowl

Paintbrush

Egg dye

Tablespoon

PVA glue

Protective glove

Kitchen towel

500 ml (18 fl oz) boiling water

1 First, wash your hands. Then, using a darning needle or cocktail stick, gently make a small hole in the shell of the egg.

2 Chip a hole in the shell just large enough to pour out the contents of the egg. Use the contents in cooking or throw them away. Gently rinse the shell in water and wash your hands.

3 Delicately remove more shell until just over half of it is left. Use your finger and thumb to gently rub or pull away as much as you can of the membrane on the inside of the shell.

Brush gently around the rim of the shell too.

4 Cover the inside and the rim of the egg shell with PVA glue, brushing lightly on the delicate shell.

5 Carefully scoop the shell into the alum (you may want to wear gloves for this). Shake it gently to cover the glued areas with alum.

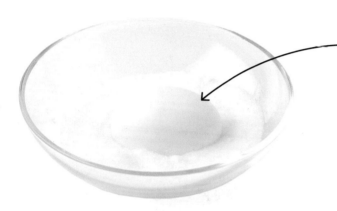

Shake off any alum that hasn't stuck to the glued areas.

6 Dip the rim in alum too, then shake off any alum that doesn't stick and leave curved-side down on kitchen towel until the glue is dry.

Handle the packet of dye carefully.

7 Ask an adult to pour the just-boiled water into the alum powder. Stir to dissolve the powder completely in the hot water, then wash your hands to make sure there's no alum on them.

8 Empty your packet of dye into the alum mix. (If you want to be sure not to accidentally dye your hands, you could wear gloves for this step.)

9 Stir the mixture until the dye has completely dissolved, then leave it to cool down.

The longer you leave the shell submerged, the more crystals will form.

10 If you aren't already wearing gloves, put them on now. Slowly lower the shell into the solution. Be careful not to splash dye around.

11 Place the shell curved-side down, level, and completely submerged on the bottom of the bowl. Leave overnight, or for at least 12 hours.

Take care – the crystals are fragile until they have dried.

12 With gloves on, carefully lift out the shell. The longer it is in the solution, the more crystals will form, so if you want more crystals, submerge the shell again for a few more hours.

Alum forms crystals as a chemical reaction with water.

13 Once you are happy with the amount of crystals on your geode, carefully put it onto kitchen paper overnight to dry fully. Throw away the gloves and alum solution, and wash your hands. Then, why not make a whole collection of geodes in eye-catching colours?

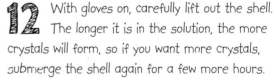

PREHISTORIC WORLD
HOW GEODES ARE FORMED

Geodes form inside holes in rock. Over time (a very, very long time!), water containing dissolved minerals can seep through into spaces and eventually crystallize on the inside surface of them. Geodes often just look like rocks from the outside, but inside is a glorious secret world of crystals. Occasionally, a whole cave becomes a giant geode, such as the one in which this person is sitting, the Pulpi Geode in Spain.

What looks like a rock from the outside may actually hide crystals inside.

COLOURFUL CRYSTALS

How a geode looks depends on the minerals in each rock cavity. Those minerals, carried by water that gradually enters the cavity, will determine what colour and shape the crystals will be. Do what nature does, and make your geodes in a whole range of beautiful colours!

Purple amethyst crystals may be formed when silicon and iron are present.

If manganese is present, crystals may have pink tones.

If the mineral celestine is present, crystals may be light blue.

Bright green crystals may be formed when copper is present.

Fine-grained quartz may form stripy blue agate.

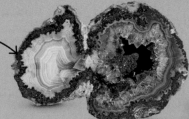

Agate comes not just in stripes, but in many colours too, depending on the other minerals present.

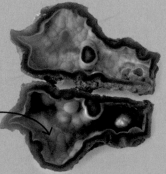

LET IT FLOW!
ERUPTING VOLCANO

Dinosaurs didn't just have to worry about being eaten by other dinosaurs. Many also had deadly volcanoes to contend with – volcanoes that at any moment might erupt to release hot, molten (liquid) rock out of the top. Create your own "erupting" volcano, but stand well back when it blows.

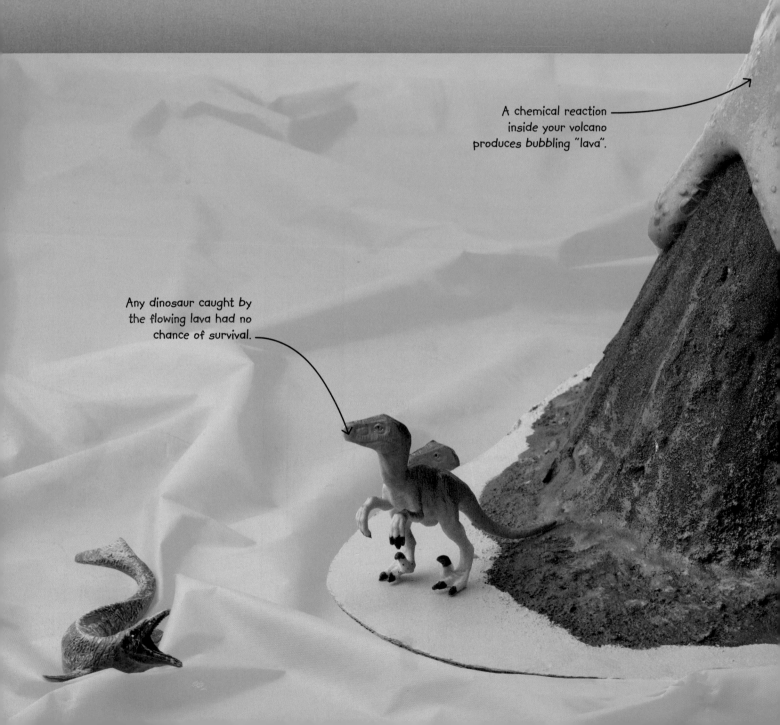

A chemical reaction inside your volcano produces bubbling "lava".

Any dinosaur caught by the flowing lava had no chance of survival.

The cone of a real volcano is made of layers of solidified lava, and it grows bigger with every eruption.

This project is messy, so work outdoors or use a plastic sheet to protect surfaces.

MAKE YOUR OWN
ERUPTING VOLCANO

Your "lava" is a foamy liquid produced by a chemical reaction using household ingredients: adding bicarbonate of soda (a base) to vinegar (containing acid) releases carbon dioxide gas bubbles that become trapped in the washing-up liquid.

Time	Difficulty	Warning
90 minutes, plus drying time	Medium	This project must be done outdoors

WHAT YOU NEED

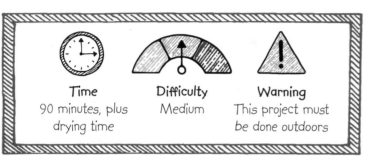

Plastic sheet

Craft card

Pencil

Tablespoon

Scissors

Large empty yoghurt pot (or other disposable container)

Washing-up liquid

Empty plastic bottle

PVA glue

Jug

Masking tape

Sand

White vinegar

Cup of water

Acrylic paints in a variety of colours

Red food colouring

Bicarbonate of soda

Paintbrushes

Stick

1 Put the plastic bottle in the middle of a piece of card and draw around it. Around the outline, sketch the shape of your "island", and cut it out.

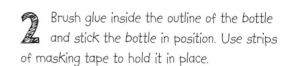

2 Brush glue inside the outline of the bottle and stick the bottle in position. Use strips of masking tape to hold it in place.

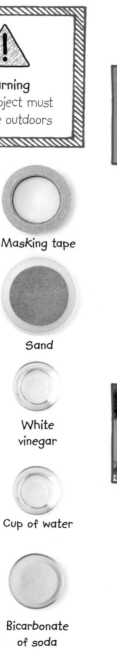

3 Cut card strips that are taller than the bottle and wider at one end than the other. Tape them around the bottle, with the wider ends at the base.

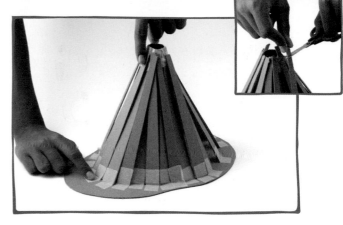

4 Continue cutting and taping strips around the bottle until you have built the basic cone shape of your volcano.

Secure the strips around the top with masking tape.

5 Add more strips to fill in the gaps, and trim off any bulky overlapping bits at the top, to keep the shape of the cone.

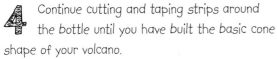

Use an empty yoghurt pot or other container you can throw away afterwards with any left-over mixture inside.

6 Wrap a final strip of masking tape around the top, then cover the whole cone with strips of masking tape to ensure there are no gaps.

7 For the "rock" mixture, pour some sand into a large yoghurt pot, add half as much glue as you have sand (a ratio of 2:1), and stir with a stick.

The opening at the top of a volcano is called the vent.

8 Add brown acrylic paint to the mixture and use the stick to work the paint completely into the mixture.

9 Paint the whole cone with the sandy mixture. Neaten the edge around the top, then leave it to dry thoroughly overnight.

Lava can *be* runny or thick – the thicker it is, the steeper the volcano.

10 Use a dark-grey colour to paint a layer of "solidified lava" around the crater that trickles down the sides towards the base too.

11 Once the grey paint is dry, dapple a green colour around the *base* to represent the plants that would grow at the foot of the volcano.

The washing-up liquid will trap the *gas bubbles* released by the chemical reaction and create foam.

12 After the green paint has dried, cover the rest of the base in sandy shades of yellow and leave it to dry.

13 Measure a tablespoon of washing-up liquid into a jug with a tablespoon of *bicarbonate* of soda. Stir them together.

Red food colouring will make your "lava" look like fiery molten rock.

14 Add two tablespoons of water to the jug and stir together. Pour the mixture into the bottle opening at the top of the volcano.

15 Measure a cup of white vinegar into a clean jug. Add a few drops of red food colouring and stir it thoroughly into the vinegar.

It's about to get messy, so stand well back as you pour.

The chemical reaction inside creates a bubbly foam that needs to escape – so it erupts out of the top!

16 Put your volcano outside, and onto some plastic sheeting to protect the surface underneath. Carefully pour the vinegar mix into the top of the bottle.

17 Watch the volcano "erupt". The lava will pour out of the volcano. When the flow starts to slow, you could add more bicarbonate of soda and vinegar to keep the eruption going.

PREHISTORIC WORLD
A WAVE OF LIQUID ROCK

Deep beneath a volcano lies a large pool of molten rock, called a magma chamber. When underground pressure builds up, magma is pushed up through the cone of the volcano to erupt and spill out as lava, as shown here on Tungarahua in Ecuador. As it erupts, a volcano can send up huge amounts of ash and smoke into the atmosphere too. It was once thought that volcanoes might have killed the dinosaurs; however, scientists are now confident that a meteorite strike was the major event.

METEORITE EXPERIMENT

Scientists think a meteorite that hit Earth 66 million years ago was probably responsible for wiping out the dinosaurs. Meteorites sometimes leave large impact craters when they hit the surface of the planet. In this experiment, you create your own craters to simulate the impact of a meteorite landing on Earth.

The way an object hits the flour and cocoa mimics the way dust and soil would fly up if a meteorite hit the Earth's surface.

Using a different-coloured powder for the surface helps show the shape and scale of the impact zone clearly.

MAKE YOUR OWN
METEORITE IMPACT SITE

In this experiment, you create your own impact craters using balls of different sizes and weights, such as a table-tennis ball, rubber ball, and marble. Find out which makes the biggest or deepest crater. Does the biggest object make the largest crater? Record the findings on your ch art. Try dropping them from higher up too, to see what happens to the crater size.

1 Fill the dish with flour and smooth it out level so that you have an even layer that is about 5 cm (2 in) deep.

Time	Difficulty
30 minutes	Easy

WHAT YOU NEED

Large dish

Tin

Long ruler or stick

Flour

Cocoa powder

Masking tape

Small sieve

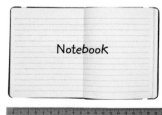

Notebook

Balls or other sphere-shaped objects to drop

Ruler

2 Use the sieve to sprinkle a thick layer of cocoa powder over the flour. Using the two colours will help you clearly see the impact zones.

Object	Small marble	Table-tennis ball	Rubber ball
Diameter of object			
Diameter of crater			
Depth of crater			
Shape of crater			

3 Prepare a chart for the results of your experiment. Make a column for each of the different "meteorites" you're going to drop.

Drop the objects from the same height, so you're measuring like-for-like.

4 Tape the long ruler to a can, and put it next to the dish. Start your experiment with the smallest "meteorite". Line it up with the top of the ruler and then drop into the dish and watch what happens on impact. Repeat with the other objects, keeping their "craters" separate.

Does your "meteorite" have a big impact on landing?

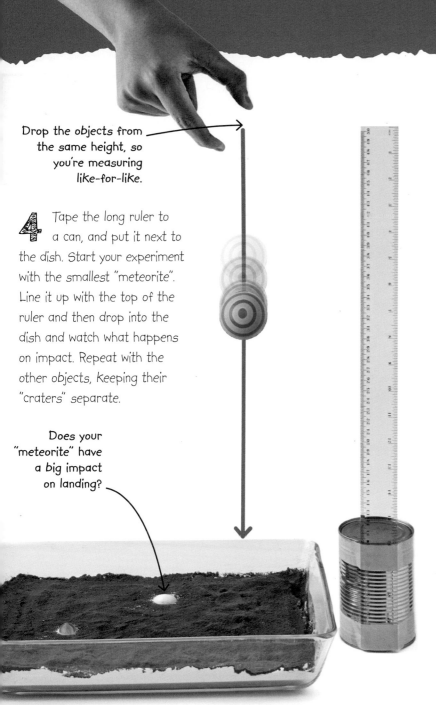

Measure the crater sizes, depth, and shapes with a ruler; what do you notice?

5 Carefully remove the "meteorites" without disturbing the craters they've made. Record the width, depth, and shape of the craters.

PREHISTORIC WORLD
A DINOSAUR-KILLER

These images show how the meteorite that hit Earth 66 million years ago may have looked as it whizzed through space, and the huge Chicxulub crater it made, 185 km (115 miles) across, as it landed. The 13-km- (8-mile-) wide meteorite would have triggered tidal waves and earthquakes, and sent up huge clouds of gases, rock, and dust that blocked out the Sun and caused ecosystems to collapse. As Earth slowly cooled, it would have become uninhabitable for most dinosaurs – only birds survived, along with some animals, such as scorpions, turtles, crocodiles, and spiders.

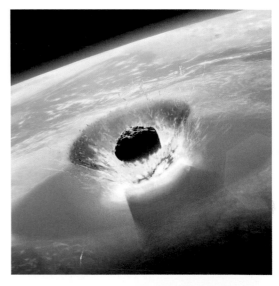

GLOSSARY

2D
See *two-dimensional*.

3D
See *three-dimensional*.

AMMONITES
Marine molluscs with a coiled shell and octopus-like tentacles that lived in Mesozoic seas.

ANGLE
The amount of turn from one direction to another. You can also think of it as the difference in direction between two lines meeting at a point. Angles are measured in degrees.

ANKYLOSAURS
Four-legged, armoured, plant-eating dinosaurs with bony studs and spikes on the neck, shoulders, and back.

ASTEROID
A space rock.

BASE
The bottom of a shape, if you imagine it sitting on a surface.

BODY FOSSIL
A fossil of the bones or shell of an actual animal.

CAM
A rotating shape that pushes or rubs against other parts of a machine to move them.

CAMSHAFT
A rod through a cam, around which the cam rotates.

CARNIVORE
An animal that eats meat.

CERATOPSIANS
Plant-eating dinosaurs, often with a bony frill at the back of the skull, such as *Triceratops*.

CONE
A 3D shape with a circular base and a single point at its top.

CONIFERS
A group of trees including pines, firs, redwoods, and cypresses.

CRETACEOUS
The era of time from 145–66 million years ago.

CYLINDER
A 3D shape that has a circle as its cross-section.

DEGREE
A measure of the size of a turn or angle. The symbol for a degree is °. A full turn is 360°.

DIAGONAL
A straight, sloping line that isn't vertical or horizontal.

EROSION
The breakdown of rock by natural forces such as water, wind, ice, or other rocks.

EXTINCTION
The dying-out of a plant or animal species.

FOSSIL
The remains of something that was once alive, preserved in rock. Teeth and bones are more likely to form fossils than softer body parts such as skin.

FOSSILIZATION
The process by which dead organisms turn into fossils.

FRICTION
A force caused by two objects that rub against each other.

GEOLOGIST
A scientist who studies rocks and minerals to find out the structure of the Earth's crust and how it formed.

GRAVITY
The force that gives everything weight and pulls things towards the ground.

HABITAT
The natural home environment of an animal or plant

HADROSAURS
Large, four-legged plant-eaters from the Cretaceous Period, many of which evolved flamboyant head crests to attract mates.

HATCHLING
A newly hatched baby animal.

HERBIVORE
An animal that eats plants.

ICHTHYOSAURS
A group of marine reptiles that first appeared in the Triassic Period. They evolved streamlined, dolphin-like bodies.

INCUBATE
To keep eggs warm so that they develop and hatch.

INTERSECT
To meet or cross over.

JURASSIC
The era of time from 201–145 million years ago.

KERATIN
A tough substance found in the feathers, hair, scales, claws, and horns of most animals.

LAVA
Molten rock that comes from a volcano; the same rock when cooled at the Earth's surface.

MAGMA
Liquid or molten rock beneath the Earth's surface.

MESOZOIC
The era of time from 252-66 million years ago.

METEORITE

An object from space, such as a rock, that lands on Earth.

OVIRAPTORIDS

Feathered, two-legged theropod dinosaurs with beaks.

PALAEONTOLOGIST

A scientist who studies the fossil remains of plants and animals.

PARALLEL

Running side by side without getting closer or further apart.

PERPENDICULAR

Something is perpendicular when it is at right angles to something else.

PISTON

A cylinder or disk that slides up and down as part of a machine.

PLESIOSAURS

Large, prehistoric marine reptiles that swam with flipper-shaped limbs. Some had very long necks and tiny heads.

PLIOSAURS

Short-necked plesiosaurs with large heads and powerful, toothed jaws.

POLYGON

Any 2D shape with three or more straight sides, such as a triangle.

POLYHEDRON

Any 3D shape whose faces are polygons.

PREDATOR

An animal that hunts and kills other animals for food.

PREY

An animal that is killed and eaten by another animal.

PROPORTION

The relative size of part of a thing compared with the whole.

PTEROSAURS

Flying reptiles that lived during the age of dinosaurs. The wings of pterosaurs consisted of sheets of skin stretched between the limbs.

RADIAL LINE

Lines that start from a central point are called radial lines.

RADIUS

Any straight line from the centre of a circle to its edge.

RATIO

Ratio compares one number or amount with another. It's written as two numbers, separated by a colon (:).

RIGHT ANGLE

An angle of 90° (a quarter turn), such as the angle between vertical and horizontal lines.

ROTATION

Turning around a central point or line.

SAUROPODS

Huge, long-necked, plant-eating dinosaurs that lived through most of the Mesozoic Era.

SCALE

The size of one thing compared to another; to copy something and make it bigger or smaller but keep all the measurements in proportion.

SEDIMENT

Small bits of weathered rock, minerals, and organic matter.

SEDIMENTARY ROCK

Rock that is formed by layers of sand and mud building up over a long time; the type of rock in which fossils are found.

SERRATED

A surface that is saw-toothed, like the edge of a bread knife.

THEROPODS

A large branch of the dinosaur family tree, made up mostly of predators. Theropods typically had sharp teeth and claws, and ranged from hen-sized creatures to the colossal *Tyrannosaurus*.

THREE-DIMENSIONAL (3D)

Having length, width, and depth. All solid objects are three-dimensional – even thin paper.

TRACE FOSSIL

A fossil made by animal activity, such as tracks, nests, or dung.

TRAPEZIUM

A four-sided two-dimensional shape with four straight sides, where two opposite sides are parallel but of unequal length and no corners are 90°.

TRIASSIC

The era of time from 252–201 million years ago.

TRILOBITES

A group of extinct marine animals without backbones.

TWO-DIMENSIONAL (2D)

Having length and width, or length and height, but no thickness.

VERTEBRAE

The bones of a skeleton that form the backbone.

WINGSPAN

The distance from the tip of one wing to the tip of the other when both wings are outstretched.

INDEX

ACKNOWLEDGMENTS

The publisher would like to thank the following people for their assistance in the preparation of this book:
Helen Peters for indexing; Dominic Elliott, Millie Hughes, Benjamin Torincsi, and Charlie Woodhouse for hand modelling; and Tanya Mehrotra for additional jacket design.

The publisher would like to thank the following for their kind permission to reproduce their photographs:

(Key: a-above; b-below/bottom; c-centre; f-far; l-left; r-right; t-top)

31 Dorling Kindersley: James Kuether (clb). 41 Science Photo Library: Mark P. Witton (br). 55 Alamy Stock Photo: Jill Stephenson (br). Dreamstime.com: Mark Turner (fbr). 61 123RF.com: Mark Turner (bl). 73 Science Photo Library: Photostock-Israel (br). 79 Dr Lida XING (br). 95 123RF.com: Leonello Calvetti (br). 107 Alamy Stock Photo: B. Christopher (br). 111 Alamy Stock Photo: Gina Rodgers (crb/Fish). Dorling Kindersley: Courtesy of Dorset Dinosaur Museum (crb). Getty Images: James L. Amos (br). 117 Alamy Stock Photo: Antonello Lanzellotto / AGF Srl (br). 121 Alamy Stock Photo: Chris Howes / Wild Places Photography (br). 125 Getty Images: Layne Kennedy / Corbis Documentary (bl). 131 Alamy Stock Photo: Ashley Lindsey (br). 141 Alamy Stock Photo: Steffen Hauser / botanikfoto (br). 147 123RF.com: fotointeractiva (ca). Alamy Stock Photo: Ingo Schulz / imageBROKER (cr). Dorling Kindersley: Natural History Museum, London (clb, bl, br). Science Photo Library: Javier Trueba / MSF (tr). 153 Dreamstime.com: Pablo Hidalgo / Pxhidalgo (br). 156 Dreamstime.com: Stocksolutions (bl, crb). 157 Alamy Stock Photo: Mark Garlick / Science Photo Library (cr); Science History Images (br)
All other images © Dorling Kindersley
For further information see: www.dkimages.com